TUCK IN CHAPS!

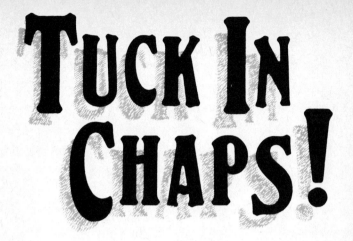

HE WAS A FIRM BELIEVER
IN CONVENIENCE FOODS

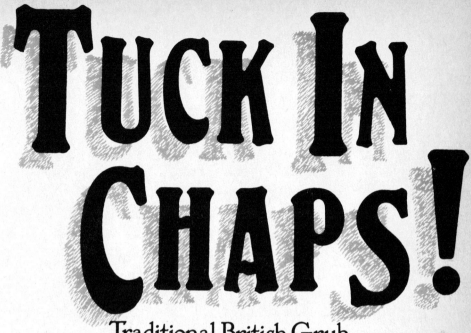

TUCK IN CHAPS!

Traditional British Grub

JANE PETTIGREW

drawings by
GLEN BAXTER

Ward Lock Limited · London

© Glen Baxter, drawings on page 1 (from *Glen Baxter: His Life*, 1983); page 6 (from *Glen Baxter: His Life*, 1983); page 9 (from *Jodhpurs in the Quantocks*, 1986); page 19 (from *Jodhpurs in the Quantocks*, 1986); page 32 (from *Atlas*, 1982); page 47 (from *The Impending Gleam*, 1981); page 63 (from *The Impending Gleam*, 1981); page 81 (from *Jodhpurs in the Quantocks*, 1986); page 109 (from *Jodhpurs in the Quantocks*, 1986); page 118 (from *The Impending Gleam*, 1981).

First published in Great Britain in 1987
by Ward Lock Limited, 8 Clifford Street
London W1X 1RB, an Egmont Company

Designed by Anita Ruddell
Additional artwork by Emma Hughes

Text filmset in Caslon
by Tradespools Limited, Frome
Printed and bound in Great Britain by Hollen Street Press

Acknowledgments
The publishers would like to thank Glen Baxter
for the drawings reproduced on pages 1, 6, 9, 19,
32, 47, 63, 81, 109 and 118.

British Library Cataloguing in Publication Data

Pettigrew, Jane
  Tuck in chaps!
  1. Cookery, English
  I. Title
  641.5942   TX717

ISBN 0-7063-6595-X

Contents

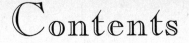

ON SUNDAYS IT WAS MY JOB
TO PREPARE A PICNIC LUNCH
USING MOTHER'S HOME-BAKED
WHOLEMEAL BREAD....

Introduction

'Tuck in Chaps!' is written for those of you who admit to growing up in the 40s and 50s (or those who wish they had!), and who remember with relish the super grub of those days; it is for anyone who would like to serve up some of those satisfying goodies but can't remember, or never knew how; it is for anyone who would like their children to indulge in the scrumptious nosh that they loved as youngsters; it is for everyone who has grown tired of nouvelle cuisine, cuisine minceur and so on (or maybe just wants a change now and then). It is for all of you who remember the spirit of the 40s and 50s, the healthy, wholesome, outdoor life of those days, cooking on camp-fires (even if it was only in the back garden!), all-day hikes with Macaroni Cheese knocked up on a wonderfully smoky fire and potatoes baked in the ashes. Stew and Dumplings, Bangers and Mash, Spotted Dick, Spam Fritters (and so many more) all go hand in hand with those days of fun and adventure. They're easy to cook, economical and absolutely first rate!

All Set For Another Busy Day

IT was the first day of the hols. Caruthers had arrived home the day before with his four chums, all very much excited by the prospect of a week of adventuring together. They would have the run of the house and grounds as Caruthers' parents had just set off on a motoring trip around France.

As the train carried them at full steam away from Mannington College, the five pals eagerly planned the week's activities. Hardcastle asked about the state of the rowing boat. 'Well,' said Caruthers, 'I haven't used it since we were all down last year. I'm sure it will need a coat of varnish and everything will have to be checked carefully.' Morrell suggested that once the boat was in good working order they could row up to Kerry's Creek and pay a visit to Captain Bates in his rambling riverside retreat. Then Bennett and Patterson suggested that the ruined tower up at Witford Heights would provide the goal for a good day's hike and Caruthers said there was a jolly good chance of a cricket match over at Westcombe. It certainly promised to be a thrilling week.

SECURING BREAKFAST WAS PROVING TO BE SOMEWHAT MORE DIFFICULT THAN I HAD AT FIRST IMAGINED

Caruthers woke at the crack of dawn and hurried to stir the others into action. If they were to get the boat ready for their trip to the Captain's, it was imperative that they make an early start. Bennett and Hardcastle set about preparing a hearty breakfast while the others gathered together the tackle they would need. Then, as they tucked into their porridge, scrambled eggs and bacon, toast and home-made apricot jam, Caruthers organized detailed plans for the day's work. Soon they were ready and set off to the boat-house.

PORRIDGE

PREPARATION AND COOKING 5–10 MINUTES
MAKES 4–5 HELPINGS

**2 cupfuls porridge oats
5 cupfuls cold water
Large pinch of salt**

Mix the ingredients together and bring to the boil. Simmer for 5 minutes, stirring from time to time. Serve with milk or cream and sugar.

Note: For a creamier porridge, use half milk and half water (2½ cupfuls of each).

FRIED EGGS,
BACON AND FRIED BREAD

PREPARATION AND COOKING 20 MINUTES
MAKES 4 HELPINGS

**8 rashers bacon
4 slices bread
oil for frying
4 eggs
Salt and freshly ground black pepper**

1   Pre-heat the oven to Gas 4/180°C/350°F and warm plates and a serving dish.

2   Put the rashers of bacon into a frying pan over a medium heat. Leave to cook gently, turning now and again so that both sides cook. Remove from the pan with a slotted spoon and keep hot on the serving dish in the oven.

3   If there is only a little bacon fat in the pan add more if you have it, otherwise a little sesame or sunflower oil. When hot, fry the slices of bread, turning once so that both sides are golden. Drain and keep hot on the serving dish.

4   Heat 2–3 tablespoons of oil in the frying pan. Break each egg one at a time into a cup and slide it gently into the hot oil. Season with a little salt and pepper and baste with spoonsful of the hot fat so that the white becomes firm and opaque and the yolk sets. Lift carefully from the pan, allowing the oil to run off. Place an egg on each slice of fried bread and serve immediately.

SCRAMBLED EGGS

PREPARATION 3 MINUTES, COOKING 10–12 MINUTES
MAKES 4 HELPINGS.

8 eggs
Salt and freshly ground black pepper
¼ pint/150 ml double cream
1½ oz/30 g butter

1   Break the eggs into a bowl, add the salt and pepper and beat lightly with a fork. Add the cream and mix well.

2   Melt the butter in a medium-sized pan. Just before it begins to sizzle, pour the eggs into the pan, reduce the heat to very low and cook slowly, stirring more or less continuously with a wooden spoon.

3   When the eggs are thickening and almost ready (this will take about 10 minutes) remove from the heat and leave in the pan for about 30 seconds so that they finish cooking in their own heat. Serve immediately.

A *few tasty variations*
To the above quantities try adding one of the following about halfway through the cooking process:

- 4 oz/100 g prawns or shrimps, drained and dried carefully.
- 4 oz/100 g chopped ham and 1 tablespoon chopped fresh chives.
- 4 oz/100 g button mushrooms, sliced and cooked gently in a little butter for 3–4 minutes.
- 4 oz/100 g chopped smoked salmon.
- 4 tomatoes, skinned, seeded and chopped, and 1 tablespoon chopped parsley.

SMOKED HADDOCK

AND BACON

PREPARATION AND COOKING 30–40 MINUTES
MAKES 5–6 HELPINGS

1½ lb/675 g smoked haddock
½ pint/300 ml milk
freshly ground black pepper
6 rashers of bacon

1   Pre-heat the oven to Gas 6/200°C/400°F. Place the haddock in a buttered casserole, sprinkle with a little pepper and pour over the milk.

2   Cover and cook for 30–40 minutes.

3   Grill the bacon and serve with the haddock.

KEDGEREE

PREPARATION AND COOKING 25–30 MINUTES
MAKES 5–6 HELPINGS

2½ oz/65 g butter
8 fl oz/220 ml boiling water
4 fl oz/110 ml long-grain white rice
½ teaspoon salt
1 lb 450 g cold smoked haddock, flaked
3 eggs
Salt and freshly ground black pepper
Large pinch of cayenne pepper

1   Pre-heat the oven to Gas 2/150°C/310°F and place a large serving dish inside to warm.

2   In a large pan, melt ½ oz/15 g of the butter. Add the rice and stir thoroughly so that all the grains are thoroughly coated with the fat. Pour in the boiling water, add the salt and stir once. Cover the pan, lower the heat, and leave entirely alone for precisely 15 minutes.

3   Meanwhile, hard-boil the eggs in a small pan for 8–10 minutes, then remove them from the pan and run cold water over them for a few minutes to prevent the yolks from blackening. Remove the shells and separate the whites from the yolks, chopping the whites and sieving the yolks.

4   Test the rice by tasting a few grains. It is ready when it is tender and has absorbed all the water. Remove from the heat.

5   Melt the remaining butter in a second large pan. Add the rice, the chopped egg-white, the flaked fish, salt and pepper and cayenne. Heat gently, stirring to stop it from sticking. When heated through, turn into the warmed serving dish and scatter the sieved egg yolk over the top. Serve immediately.

CAMP BREAD

PREPARATION 40 MINUTES, COOKING 3–4 MINUTES EACH SLICE
MAKES 5–6 HELPINGS

**6 slices white bread
4 oz/100 g plain flour
pinch of salt
1 egg, beaten
4 fl oz/90 ml milk
Oil or fat for frying**

1   To make the batter, place the flour and salt in a bowl and make a well in the middle. Pour the egg into the well, add a little milk, and gradually mix the flour into the egg, working it down from the sides of the bowl. Gradually add the rest of the milk. Beat well and leave to stand for 30 minutes.

2   Cut the crusts off the bread and cut each slice into two. Heat the fat or oil in a frying pan. Dip each piece of bread in batter to coat it and place carefully in the hot fat. Fry, turning once, until both sides are golden.

3   Remove carefully with a slotted spoon and drain on kitchen towel. Serve hot with tomato ketchup and camp-fire things such as sausages and bacon and eggs.

BREGG

PREPARATION 5 MINUTES, COOKING 4–5 MINUTES FOR EACH PIECE
MAKES 5–6 HELPINGS

**6 slices white bread, crusts removed
6 tablespoons milk
3 eggs
Salt and freshly ground black pepper
Butter or oil for frying**

1   Beat the eggs with the milk and season with salt and pepper.

2   Cut each slice of bread into two and lay in the beaten egg mixture. Leave for a couple of minutes to soak.

3   Heat the butter or oil in a frying pan and fry the soaked bread, turning carefully until golden brown on both sides. Remove from the pan and serve immediately, with bacon, sausages, grilled tomatoes etc.

POACHED EGGS

PREPARATION AND COOKING 5–6 MINUTES
MAKES 4 HELPINGS.

½ teaspoon salt
1 pint/600 ml water
1 teaspoon lemon juice
4 eggs
4 slices buttered toast

1   Bring the water to the boil in a frying pan then add the salt and the lemon juice and reduce the heat so that the water is just simmering.

2   Break each egg one at a time into a cup, taking great care not to break the yolk, then gently slide into the water.

3   Leave to cook for about 3 minutes or until the white around the yolk can be touched without breaking. Carefully remove the egg from the pan with a slotted spoon or spatula and lay on a piece of buttered toast.

Variation: Hardcastle's Cheesy Eggs
Hardcastle learnt this capital version of poached eggs from his uncle's butler, Jenkins.

1   Prepare the eggs as for poached eggs and lay on slices of buttered toast.

2   Sprinkle 1 oz/25 g of grated mature cheddar on top of each egg. Season with salt and a little black pepper and brown under the grill.

KIPPERS

PREPARATION AND COOKING 20–25 MINUTES
MAKES 4 HELPINGS

4 very fresh kippers
2 oz/50 g butter, melted

1   Place the kippers in hot water to cover for 1–2 minutes, then lift out and dry carefully with paper towel.

2   Place the kippers in the grill pan, skin side down, and brush with the melted butter. Grill gently for 10–15 minutes, then turn and cook the underside for a further 10–15 minutes. Just before serving spread with a little cold butter.

Note: If you like a good strong smoky flavour to your kipper omit the soak in hot water; just spread with butter and grill.

DEVILLED KIDNEYS

This mildly spicy breakfast treat has been a favourite of our five pals ever since Hardcastle's uncle, Major George Dawson (who spent many years in Northern India and who is therefore an experienced curry eater) knocked it up for them one morning during one of their customary visits to his country residence in Wiltshire. The chums found it an excellent alternative to bacon and eggs.

•

PREPARATION AND COOKING 35–40 MINUTES
MAKES 3–4 HELPINGS

12 lamb's kidneys
2 oz/50 g butter
2 teaspoons mild curry powder
Salt and freshly ground black pepper
1 oz/25 g plain flour
5 fl oz/150 ml milk
5 fl oz/150 ml double cream
4 slices buttered toast

1   Prepare the kidneys as described on page 17.

2   Melt the butter in a pan, add the curry powder, salt and pepper and the kidneys and cook gently for 4–5 minutes, turning so that both sides cook. Remove from the pan with a slotted spoon and place in a dish.

3   Add the flour to the juice in the pan and mix carefully. Stir over a gentle heat for 1 minute. Remove the pan from the heat and gradually add the milk, mixing carefully. Place the pan back on the stove and cook for 1–2 minutes, stirring all the time.

4   Add the cream and mix well. Replace the kidneys in the sauce and cook gently for 20–25 minutes. Spoon onto hot buttered toast and serve immediately.

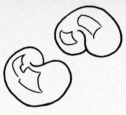

GRILLED KIDNEYS

PREPARATION AND COOKING 10–15 MINUTES
MAKES 5–6 HELPINGS

12 lamb's kidneys
2 oz/50 g butter
Salt and freshly ground black pepper
6 slices buttered toast
2 oz/50 g Maître d'hôtel butter (see below)

To make Maître d'hôtel butter
2 oz/50 g butter, softened
2 teaspoons finely chopped parsley
2 teaspoons lemon juice
Salt and freshly ground black pepper

Mix all the ingredients together and beat hard for a minute. Spread onto a plate and leave in the refrigerator to harden.

1   Pre-heat the oven to Gas 2/150°C/310°F and warm the plates.

2   Prepare the kidneys as described in the recipe opposite, but remove the central core without cutting right through them. Place them in a small pan and cover with boiling water. Leave in the water for 2 minutes, then drain, and thread the open kidneys carefully onto wooden or metal skewers.

3   Melt the butter and brush carefully over the kidneys. Season with salt and pepper and place under a hot grill, cut side uppermost. Cook for 3–4 minutes, depending on size, then turn and grill for a further 3–4 minutes.

4   Place 2–3 kidneys on each slice of buttered toast with a small pat of Maître d'hôtel butter on the middle of each kidney.

KIDNEYS ON TOAST

PREPARATION AND COOKING 25–30 MINUTES
MAKES 5–6 HELPINGS

**10 lamb's kidneys
2 oz/50 g butter, softened
1 teaspoon lemon juice
Large pinch of cayenne pepper
Salt and freshly ground black pepper
5–6 slices buttered toast**

1   Prepare the kidneys (see below), place them in a small pan and add enough water to just cover. Bring to the boil, lower the heat and simmer for 15–20 minutes.

2   Remove the kidneys from the pan and put them in a food processor or blender with the butter, lemon juice, cayenne pepper, salt and black pepper. Blend thoroughly. If you don't have a blender or processor, press them through a strong wire sieve and beat them together with the other ingredients using a wooden spoon.

3   Spread the kidney mixture on to the buttered toast and serve immediately.

Preparing kidneys

Kidneys are sometimes sold in a solid layer of fat or membrane which must be removed before cooking. It is also necessary to remove the central core. To do this, cut the kidney in half lengthways and snip out the white part with scissors or a sharp knife.

BOILED EGGS

WITH 'SOLDIER BOYS'

Place the eggs in a pan containing enough boiling water to completely cover them. Leave to cook for the following number of minutes according to taste:

- To boil lightly so that the whites are slightly liquid – 3 minutes.
- To cook so that the whites are slightly soft – 3½ minutes.
- To cook so that the whites are firm but the yolk is runny – 4–4½ minutes.
- To hard boil 8–10 minutes.

For 'soldier boys' simply spread thin slices of bread with plenty of butter and cut each slice into 4 or 5 fingers.

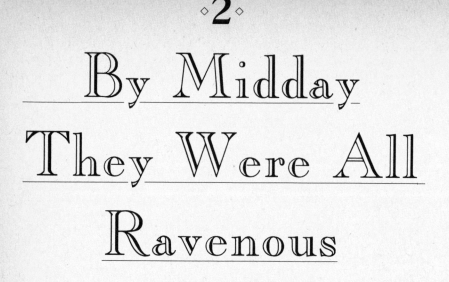

◇2◇

By Midday They Were All Ravenous

THEY worked hard all morning, pausing only to watch the local rowing club practising their skills against the river's strong currents. They didn't even notice the time until suddenly Morrell exclaimed, 'By jove, I'm absolutely starved. How about some grub?' 'Right,' said Caruthers, 'Why don't two of you jog up to the village and get some supplies? Maybe you could rustle something up for lunch while we finish off here. Let's meet up at the house in about 45 minutes!'

Hardcastle and Patterson volunteered, leaving the others to finish repairing the rudder. As they headed off towards the village, Caruthers called after them, 'I say, you fellows. See if you can get some of those first-rate sausages that Mater sometimes packs in my hamper – we could have bangers and mash.' 'Righto,' called Hardcastle, 'we'll see what we can do.'

Just over an hour later they were all seated around the large kitchen table, eagerly devouring an enormous mountain of steaming mashed potatoes and deliciously spicy fat sausages.

'Super grub, you two,' said Morrell. This will really set us up for a good afternoon's work!'

WALMSLEY SEEMED TO BE EXPERIENCING
SOME DIFFICULTY
WITH THE SEAFOOD SALAD

BAKED SPUDS

WITH CHEESE AND BACON

PREPARATION 10 MINUTES, COOKING 2 HOURS
MAKES 6 HELPINGS

6 large potatoes
4 oz/100 g streaky or other bacon
4 oz/100 g mature Cheddar, grated
Salt and freshly ground black pepper
½ teaspoon ground nutmeg

1   Pre-heat the oven to Gas 5/190°C/375°F.

2   Scrub, rinse and dry the potatoes and cut through the skin on the upper part of each one to give the appearance of a lid. Bake for about 1½ hours or until they feel tender when gently squeezed.

3   Meanwhile fry or grill the bacon till crispy, then cut into small pieces.

4   When the potatoes have cooled slightly, carefully cut off the lids. Scoop out the potato, including the inside of the lids, taking care not to split the skins. Mash the potato in a bowl. Keep back about 4 tablespoons of cheese to sprinkle on top, and mix the rest into the mashed potato, with the bacon, black pepper and nutmeg.

5   Pile the mixture back into the skins and sprinkle the remaining cheese on top. Return to the oven and bake for a further 15–20 minutes till thoroughly hot and golden brown. Serve immediately.

SPAM FRITTERS

PREPARATION 35 MINUTES, COOKING 3–4 MINUTES FOR EACH FRITTER
MAKES 4

1 tin spam
4 oz/100 g plain flour
Pinch of salt
1 egg, beaten
4 fl oz/90 ml milk
Fat or oil for frying

1   Slice the spam into 4 slices.

2   Mix the batter as for fritters (see page 28) and leave to stand for 30 minutes.

3   Heat about ½ in/1 cm of fat or oil in a frying pan, and when it begins to smoke coat the slices of spam with the batter and place carefully one by one into the hot fat. Fry on both sides until golden brown.

MACARONI CHEESE

PREPARATION AND COOKING 40–45 MINUTES
MAKES 5–6 HELPINGS

**8 oz/225 g macaroni or similar pasta
2 oz/50 g butter
2 oz/50 g plain flour
1 pint/600 ml milk
8 oz/225 g mature Cheddar, grated
Salt and freshly ground black pepper
Good pinch of cayenne pepper**

1   Pre-heat the oven to Gas 5/190°C/375°F and warm a serving dish or casserole and the plates. Place the macaroni in a large pan with plenty of cold water, add 1 teaspoon salt and bring to the boil. Boil for 15–20 minutes, or until just tender, without covering the pan. Drain.

2   Meanwhile make the cheese sauce. Melt the butter in a medium-sized pan. Stir the flour into the butter and cook, stirring constantly, for 2–3 minutes. Remove from the heat and gradually add the milk, stirring carefully.

3   Return to the heat and stir briskly until the sauce thickens. Add two-thirds of the grated cheese, salt and pepper to taste, and the cayenne pepper.

4   Mix the macaroni into the sauce and turn into the serving dish or casserole. Sprinkle the remaining cheese over the top and bake for 15–20 minutes until golden brown.

Variations
- Just before placing in the oven, put slices of tomato over the top with a small pat of butter on each one.
- Removing the rinds from some bacon rashers, roll them up and bake in a baking tin while the macaroni cheese is browning. Use to garnish.

CAULIFLOWER CHEESE

PREPARATION AND COOKING 25–30 MINUTES
MAKES 4–5 HELPINGS

**1 large cauliflower
Salt and freshly ground black pepper
2 oz/50 g butter
2 oz/50 g plain flour
1 pint/600 ml milk
A pinch of nutmeg
8 oz/225 g mature cheddar, grated**

1   Pre-heat the oven to Gas 5/190°C/375°F and warm a serving dish and plates.

2   Break the cauliflower into florets, trimming off any hard stalk and leaves. Place in a pan with just enough water to cover, add 1 teaspoon salt and bring to the boil. Reduce heat and simmer for about 5 minutes, until just beginning to soften. Drain and place in the serving dish in the oven to keep hot.

3   Meanwhile, make the cheese sauce. Melt the butter in a medium-sized pan. Stir the flour into the butter and cook, stirring constantly, for 2–3 minutes. Remove from the heat and gradually add the milk, stirring carefully.

4   Return to the heat and stir briskly until the sauce thickens, then add three-quarters of the grated cheese, reserving the rest to sprinkle on top. Stir until the cheese has melted, then season with black pepper and nutmeg.

5   Pour the sauce over the cauliflower, scatter the remaining cheese on top and return to the oven. Cook for a further 15–20 minutes until the top is golden brown. Serve immediately.

Variation
Instead of using all milk for the sauce, use half milk and half cauliflower stock.

WELSH RAREBIT

PREPARATION AND COOKING 15–20 MINUTES
MAKES 4 HELPINGS

6 oz/175 g mature Cheddar, grated
Freshly ground black pepper
1 teaspoon whole-grain mustard
½ teaspoon creamed horseradish
Few drops of Worcester sauce
2 tablespoon milk or cream
4 slices buttered toast, to serve

Mix together all the ingredients and blend thoroughly. Pile onto the buttered toast and brown under the grill. Serve immediately.

Variations

- *Buck Rarebit* Make as above but top each slice of cooked rarebit with a poached egg. Serve immediately.
- *Yorkshire Rarebit* Remove the rind from 4 rashers of bacon, grill them, and place on top of the cooked rarebit. Alternatively, chop the cooked bacon and add to the rarebit mixture before spreading onto the toast.
- *Scotch Rarebit* Put 8 oz/225 g Stilton or Cheshire cheese in a saucepan with 1 oz/25 g butter, a wine-glass of stout, 1 heaped teaspoon made mustard and a little black pepper. Stir over a low heat until the mixture resembles thick cream. Spoon onto the slices of buttered toast and brown lightly under the grill. Alternatively serve the mixture in a hot dish and serve the buttered toast separately.

BUBBLE AND SQUEAK

PREPARATION 5 MINUTES, COOKING 20 MINUTES
MAKES 4 HELPINGS

1 lb/450 g left-over cold roast or boiled beef
1 white cabbage
Salt and freshly ground black pepper
3 oz/75 g butter

1   Clean and chop the cabbage and place in a saucepan with enough water to just cover. Add 1 teaspoon salt, bring to the boil, then reduce the heat and simmer for 5–7 minutes. Drain well.

2   Pre-heat the oven to Gas 2/150°C/310°F and warm a serving dish and plates. Melt 1½ oz of the butter in a saucepan and toss the cabbage in it until well coated. Leave on a gentle heat.

3   Cut the meat into small strips or pieces. Melt the remaining butter in a second saucepan or frying pan and toss the meat in the butter with salt and black pepper to taste. Heat through.

4   When both meat and cabbage are well heated, pile the cabbage in the middle of the dish and arrange the meat around it. Serve immediately.

RISSOLES

PREPARATION AND COOKING 30–40 MINUTES
MAKES 8

8 oz/225 g cooked left-over meat (beef, lamb, chicken etc)
8 oz/225 g left-over mashed potato
1 tablespoon tomato ketchup
1 teaspoon chopped fresh parsley
1 large egg, beaten and 1 egg yolk, beaten
Salt and freshly ground black pepper
3 oz/75 g plain flour
Golden breadcrumbs for coating
Fat or oil for frying

1   Mince the meat very finely or place in the food processor for 1 minute.

2   Mix together the meat, potato, ketchup, parsley, egg yolk, salt and pepper, making sure the ingredients are evenly distributed.

3   Shape into round flat cakes, working with floured hands. Toss in flour, dip in the beaten egg, then roll in the breadcrumbs.

4   Heat the fat or oil in a frying pan and fry the rissoles until well browned on both sides. Serve with relish or chutney.

CHEESY ONIONS

PREPARATION AND COOKING 35–40 MINUTES
MAKES 4–5 HELPINGS

**2½ lb/1.125 kg onions, peeled
Salt and freshly ground black pepper
2 oz/50 g butter
2 oz/50 g plain flour
1 pint/600 ml milk
8 oz/225 g mature Cheddar
1 tablespoon chopped fresh parsley**

1   Pre-heat the oven to Gas 5/190°C/375°F and warm a serving dish and plates.

2   Cut the onions into quarters, then place in a pan with enough water to cover, add 1 teaspoon salt and bring to the boil. Reduce heat and simmer for 10–15 minutes until just tender. Drain carefully and place in the serving dish in the oven to keep hot.

3   Meanwhile put aside one-third of the cheese to sprinkle on top, and make the cheese sauce as in the recipe on the previous page, but omitting the nutmeg. Season with salt and black pepper and add the parsley.

4   Pour the sauce over the onions, scatter the remaining cheese on top and return to the oven. Cook for a further 15–20 minutes until the top is golden brown.

Variations
- Instead of using all milk for the sauce, use half milk and half onion stock.
- Try adding 3–4 hard-boiled eggs, shelled and halved, to the sauce before the final oven cooking.

MUSHROOM OMELETTE

PREPARATION AND COOKING 30 MINUTES
MAKES 2 HELPINGS

**8 oz/225 g mushrooms
2 oz/50 g butter
1 tablespoon chopped fresh parsley
Salt and freshly ground black pepper
4 large eggs, separated**

1   Wipe the mushrooms, carefully trim the stalks and slice. Melt 1 oz/
25 g of the butter in a medium-sized pan. Add the mushrooms, parsley,
salt and pepper and cook gently for 10–15 minutes.

2   Meanwhile prepare the eggs. To the yolks, add half an egg-shell of
water for each egg and beat with a wooden spoon until creamy.

3   Whisk the whites until stiff, then gently fold into the yolks. Slowly
heat the remaining butter in a large, thick frying pan without allowing it
to brown.

4   Pour the egg mixture into the pan and cook until golden brown on
the underside. Meanwhile heat the grill. When the omelette is golden
underneath place the pan under the grill and lightly brown the top.

5   Lift the mushrooms from their pan with a slotted spoon and spread
over one half of the omelette. Run a palette knife around the edge of the
pan, fold the omelette over and serve immediately.

Variations
- Instead of mushrooms, use 4 oz/100 g chopped ham mixed with 2 oz/
  50 g cooked peas.
- Add 4 lamb's kidneys, trimmed and cut into small pieces, then sautéed
  in a little butter with a small chopped onion.
- Add 6 oz/175 g shrimps or prawns heated in a little butter with 2–3
  chopped spring onions and a pinch of cayenne.
- Make a mixture of 2 oz/50 g of chopped ham, 1 green or red pepper,
  one chopped onion and 2–3 tomatoes. Sauté in a little butter until the
  vegetables are tender and add to the omelette.

MUSHROOMS ON TOAST

PREPARATION AND COOKING 20 MINUTES
MAKES 4–5 HELPINGS

**1½ lb/675 g mushrooms
1 oz/25 g butter
½ teaspoon dried tarragon
Salt and freshly ground black pepper
1 oz/25 g plain flour
½ pint/300 ml double cream
4–5 slices buttered toast**

1   Pre-heat the oven to Gas 4/180°C/350°F. Wipe the mushrooms carefully and trim the stalks.

2   Melt the butter in a medium-sized pan and add the mushrooms, tarragon, salt and pepper. Cook very gently for 10 minutes. Remove the mushrooms with a slotted spoon and keep warm in the oven.

3   Add the flour to the butter and juice in the pan, mixing carefully. Allow to cook for 2–3 minutes, then carefully add the cream, a little at a time. Cook gently until the mixture thickens, then return the mushrooms to the pan and heat gently through. Serve on the slices of buttered toast.

CREAMED SWEETBREADS

PREPARATION 1¼ HOURS, COOKING 30 MINUTES
MAKES 4 HELPINGS

**12 oz–1 lb/350–540 g sweetbreads
4 fl oz/110 ml stock, or milk and stock mixed
A little lemon juice
Salt and freshly ground black pepper
1 oz/25 g plain flour
1 tablespoon milk
2 tablespoons double cream**

1   Soak the sweetbreads in cold water for 1 hour. Drain and then place in a saucepan and cover with fresh clean water. Bring to the boil, then drain thoroughly and leave to cool a little.

2   Trim off any skin and fat and cut into neat pieces about 1 in/2.5 cm thick. Place in a pan with the stock or milk and stock, lemon juice and salt and pepper. Simmer gently for about 15–20 minutes. Remove the sweetbreads and lay in a warmed serving dish. Keep warm in the oven.

3   Blend the flour with the 1 tablespoon of milk, add the stock, then bring to the boil. Cook, stirring constantly, until the sauce has thickened. Stir in the cream and pour over the sweetbreads. Serve immediately.

FRITTERS

These are jolly tasty served with bacon, fried tomatoes, mushrooms, sausages or fried eggs.

•

PREPARATION 35 MINUTES, COOKING 3–4 MINUTES FOR EACH FRITTER
MAKES 9–10

4 oz/100 g plain flour
Pinch of salt
1 egg, beaten
4 fl oz/85–90 ml milk
Fat or oil for frying

1 Place the flour and salt in a bowl and mix together. Make a well in the middle and pour the egg into the well. Add 3–4 tablespoons milk and gradually mix the flour into the egg and milk, working the flour down from the sides and adding more milk as required. Beat well, and then leave to stand for 30 minutes.

2 Heat ½ in/1 cm of fat or oil in a frying pan until it just begins to smoke. Carefully place spoonfuls of batter one at a time into the hot fat. When golden on one side, turn and cook the other side. Lift carefully out with a slotted spoon and drain on paper towel. Serve immediately.

Variation: Bennett's Favourite Fritters

These were invented by the resourceful Bennett while on a hiking expedition with Hardcastle. When it came to preparing their well-earned midday refreshment they realized with horror that they had only brought along one pan in which to fry.

They had with them sausages, bacon, dripping and all the necessary ingredients for fritters (a firm favourite of the chums). They very quickly realized that it would be quite impossible to cook the sausages and bacon and keep them hot while they concerned themselves with the fritters, so Bennett, with a sudden flash of inspiration, suggested that having cooked the meat items, they should chop them up, mix them with the batter and fry the delicious concoction as bacon and sausage fritters. After achieving this, and having enormously enjoyed them, the pals decided it really was the only way to eat fritters. They also decided that such fritters are enhanced no end by a generous blob of tomato ketchup.

THE FOLLOWING AMOUNTS WILL MAKE 10–12 FRITTERS

4 rashers of bacon – fried and chopped
4 spicy sausages – fried and chopped into ½-in/1-cm chunks
Batter mixture as above

Mix the chopped meats into the batter mixture so that the pieces are all well coated. Spoon the fritters carefully into the pan of hot fat as before.

CORNED BEEF HASH

This camp-fire delicacy is also known as 'Slosh' by our five adventurers, for obvious reasons! If ever in short supply of ideas about what to cook for their lunch or supper the five's first reaction is to raid the stores in search of surplus tins of corned beef and a couple of pounds of spuds.

●

PREPARATION AND COOKING 45–55 MINUTES
MAKES 4–5 HELPINGS

**2½ lb/1.25 kg potatoes
Salt and freshly ground black pepper
1 × 12 oz/340 g tin corned beef
Oil or butter for frying**

1   Heat the oven to Gas 4/180°C/350°F and warm a serving dish and plates.

2   Peel the potatoes and cut into small pieces. Place in a medium-sized saucepan with enough cold water to just cover, add 1 teaspoon salt and bring to the boil. Reduce heat and simmer for 10–15 minutes until tender but not mushy.

3   Drain and mash with black pepper. Beat well until smooth and well mixed.

4   Open the tin of corned beef and break up into small pieces. Add to the potato and mix thoroughly so that the meat is evenly distributed.

5   Heat the oil or butter in a frying pan. Add as much of the potato and meat mixture as will fit into the pan, like a large pancake. Leave to brown on one side, then turn and brown the other side. Slide into the serving dish and keep warm in the oven. If the mixture did not all fit the first time, repeat the process with the remainder. When it is all cooked serve with tomato relish or ketchup.

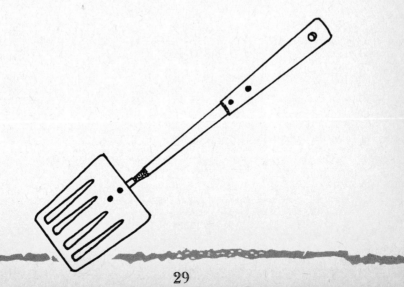

BANGERS AND MASH

PREPARATION 10–15 MINUTES, COOKING 20 MINUTES
MAKES 5–6 HELPINGS

12 sausages
3 lb/1.35 kg potatoes
1 teaspoon salt
3 oz/75 g butter
2 tablespoons milk
2 tablespoons cream
Freshly ground pepper

1   Pre-heat the oven to Gas 3/170°C/325°F and warm a serving dish and plates.

2   Fry or grill the sausages gently until brown all over and thoroughly cooked.

3   Meanwhile peel the potatoes and cut into pieces. Place in a saucepan with enough cold water to cover, add the salt and bring to the boil. Reduce the heat and simmer for about 15 minutes or until soft.

4   Drain the potatoes and break them up with a fork or masher. Add the butter, milk, cream and black pepper and beat thoroughly until fluffy.

5   Spoon the potato onto the serving dish, arrange the sausages on top and serve immediately.

BOMBAY TOAST

PREPARATION AND COOKING 20 MINUTES
MAKES 4 HELPINGS

4 medium eggs
4 tablespoons double cream
¾ teaspoon anchovy essence
24 capers, 12 chopped, 12 left whole
Salt and freshly ground black pepper
A good shake of cayenne pepper
1 oz/25 g butter
4 slices buttered toast
4 anchovy fillets, cut into thin strips

1   Beat the eggs well in a bowl. Add the cream, anchovy essence and chopped capers and mix well. Season with salt, pepper and cayenne.

2   Melt the butter in a small pan and add the egg mixture. Cook gently over a low heat, stirring frequently. When cooked, pile on to the toast.

3   Lay the strips of anchovy fillet across the top of the egg to form a lattice pattern. Place a whole caper in between the fillets and serve.

FISH CAKES

PREPARATION AND COOKING 1 HOUR (ALLOWING TIME FOR MIXTURE TO COOL BEFORE
FORMING CAKES)
MAKES 16–18

1½ lb/675 g potatoes
Salt and freshly ground black pepper
1 lb/450 g cooked cod or haddock
1 oz/25 g butter or margarine
2 eggs, separated
2 tablespoons chopped fresh parsley
Golden breadcrumbs for coating
Oil for frying
A little flour

1   Peel the potatoes and cut into small pieces. Place in a medium-sized saucepan with enough cold water to cover, add ½ teaspoon salt and bring to the boil. Reduce heat and simmer for 10–15 minutes until tender but not mushy. Drain and mash.

2   Remove any skin and bones from the fish and chop coarsely. Heat the butter in a pan, add the fish, the potatoes, the yolk of 1 egg, salt and black pepper to taste, and the parsley. Stir over the heat for a few minutes, then remove from the heat and leave to cool.

3   When cool enough to handle, shape the mixture into round flat cakes, working with floured hands.

4   Beat the second egg with the remaining egg white and brush over the cakes. Coat with breadcrumbs and fry in hot fat until both sides are golden brown. Serve immediately.

Tea Around The Fire

EVERY OTHER WEDNESDAY THE LADS
WERE ALLOWED AN EXTRA RATION

IT was a rotten blustering day. The rain had been falling relentlessly since mid-morning and the chums had given up all hope of their planned hike. Caruthers suggested that they should brighten the afternoon by having a slap-up tea around the fire with crumpets and muffins and toast and cakes. They all agreed heartily that this was a fine idea and Caruthers went off to the kitchen.

As he searched in the larder for the necessary goodies he was reminded of an amusing incident at Mannington only a few weeks before, and he chuckled to himself as he remembered the sudden and unexpected visit he had received from his house captain one Sunday afternoon. Fairbairn had entered with his face full of anxiety and his voice full of concern, saying 'Do you happen to have a pot of jam you could lend me?' Caruthers had fairly staggered at such an unexpected request. 'A pot of jam!' he had exclaimed, 'whatever do you mean?' 'Any sort will do', said the captain, still looking most anxious and concerned, 'and I suppose you haven't got a cake of any kind, or some muffins or . . . ' He stopped, suddenly understanding why Caruthers was looking at him so inquisitively. 'What an ass I am! I forgot to explain myself. The fact is, I asked a couple of new boys up for tea this afternoon and I've just remembered I have nothing but tea and toast to offer them – and as it's Sunday I can't go out and get anything in. I'd be awfully obliged if you could help me out.'

Caruthers offered Fairbairn anything he could find in his cupboard, and the captain availed himself of the offer to secure a pot of home-made strawberry jam, a small jar of potted meat, half a dozen muffins, a few Eccles cakes and a considerable portion of plum cake.

SANDWICHES

TOASTED BACON

PREPARATION AND COOKING 10–15 MINUTES
MAKES 2 ROUNDS

5–6 rashers streaky bacon, rinds removed
1½ oz/40 g butter

1   Grill or fry the bacon until crispy. Keep hot in the oven or at one end of the grill pan.

2   Toast the slices of bread on one side only.

3   Butter the untoasted sides of the bread. Lay the bacon on two of the slices, put the other two slices on top, and eat immediately.

CHEESE AND CHUTNEY

The best chutneys for this sandwich are peach, mango, curried fruit, apricot and sultana or similar.

PREPARATION 5 MINUTES
MAKES 4 ROUNDS

1 tablespoon chopped fresh chives
8 oz/225 g mature Cheddar, grated
2–3 tablespoons chutney

Spread slices of bread with chutney. Scatter over a few chives, then pile the grated cheese on top. Cover with the other slices of bread. Press well together and cut in halves or quarters.

CHOCOLATE SPREAD
WITH HUNDREDS AND THOUSANDS

Butter slices of white bread. Spread a layer of chocolate spread on half the slices. Sprinkle a generous layer of hundreds and thousands on top, then press the other slices of bread on top. Cut into squares or triangles.

CREAM CHEESE AND DATE

PREPARATION 5 MINUTES
MAKES 4 ROUNDS

**6 oz/175 g cream cheese, softened
3–4 oz/75–100 g plump, dried dates, stoned and chopped**

Cover a slice of buttered or unbuttered bread generously with cream cheese, lay chopped dates on top, and press down another slice of bread firmly. Cut into squares or triangles.

EGG AND ANCHOVY

PREPARATION 10 MINUTES
MAKES 4 ROUNDS

**20 anchovies, washed and boned
6 hard-boiled egg yolks
2 oz/50 g grated parmesan or cheddar
Pinch of cayenne pepper
2–3 tablespoons double cream**

1 Mix together all the ingredients and beat or blend until creamy.

2 Spread onto buttered or unbuttered bread, top with another slice of bread, trim off the crusts and cut into fingers.

HAM AND CUCUMBER

PREPARATION 4–5 MINUTES
MAKES 4 ROUNDS

**⅔ cucumber, peeled and sliced thinly
Salt and freshly ground black pepper
1 teaspoon freshly squeezed lemon juice
8 oz/225 g sliced ham**

1 Place the sliced cucumber in a dish with the salt, pepper and lemon juice, turning it in the seasoning so that each slice is coated.

2 Lay the slices of ham on buttered bread and arrange the cucumber on top. Put on another slice of bread on top, press down, trim off the crusts and cut into triangles.

TURKEY AND CRANBERRY

PREPARATION 3 MINUTES
MAKES 4 ROUNDS

**4 teaspoons cranberry jelly
8 oz/225 g cold cooked turkey, sliced
Mustard if liked
Salt and freshly ground black pepper**

Spread a little mustard, if using, on buttered bread. Spread on the cranberry jelly, lay the pieces of turkey on top, then press on another slice of bread, trim off the crusts and cut into squares or triangles.

TUNA AND CUCUMBER

PREPARATION 4–5 MINUTES,
MAKES 4 ROUNDS

**1 × 7-oz/198-g tin of tuna in oil, drained
1 teaspoon freshly squeezed lemon juice or cider vinegar
Salt and freshly ground black pepper
⅔ cucumber, peeled and thinly sliced**

1   Mash the fish with a fork, add the lemon juice or vinegar, salt and pepper and mix thoroughly.

2   Spread the fish on buttered bread and arrange the cucumber over the top. Sprinkle a little more salt and pepper on the cucumber. Press another slice of bread carefully on top, trim off the crusts and cut into squares or triangles.

Variation:
In summer, chop up a few fresh mint leaves and mix with the tuna.

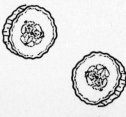

POTTED BEEF

PREPARATION AND COOKING 1¼ HOURS
MAKES ENOUGH FOR 4 SLICES OF TOAST

8 oz/200 g steak
Salt and freshly ground black pepper
½ teaspoon mixed spice
1½ teaspoons anchovy essence
2 teaspoons double cream
Clarified butter (see below)

1   Cut the meat into small pieces, place it in a saucepan with a little salt and enough water to just cover. Bring to the boil and simmer gently for about 1 hour until the flesh will separate easily with a fork.

2   Strain off the juice and reserve. Put the meat in a food processor with the other ingredients and blend well together. Alternatively put the meat through the mincer then mix with the other ingredients with a fork or wooden spoon. Add a little of the reserved juice to moisten.

3   Put the meat into ramekins or similar small dishes. When cold pour a little clarified butter over each one.

To make clarified butter
Place the required amount of butter in a saucepan. Heat very slowly and remove the scum as it rises. When the butter is quite clear, pour immediately over the beef or whatever is being potted.

SARDINES ON TOAST

PREPARATION 7–8 MINUTES
MAKES ENOUGH FOR 2 SLICES

1 × 4.37-oz/124-g tin sardines
Pinch of cayenne pepper
1 teaspoon Worcester sauce
1 teaspoon lemon juice
2 slices of buttered brown or white toast

1   Remove the bones from the sardines and mash the flesh thoroughly. Add the other ingredients then spread onto the toast.

2   Place under a hot grill for 2–3 minutes until just beginning to sizzle. Serve immediately.

CINNAMON TOAST

PREPARATION AND COOKING 12–13 MINUTES
MAKES 4 SLICES (12 FINGERS)

**4 slices of thin white bread, crusts removed
1½ oz/40 g unsalted butter, softened
4 tablespoons icing sugar
1½ teaspoon ground cinnamon**

1   Pre-heat the oven to Gas 6/200°C/400°F.

2   Beat together the butter, sugar and cinnamon until light and creamy. Spread onto the bread and cut each slice into 3 fingers.

3   Place on a baking tray and bake for 7–8 minutes.

CRUMPETS AND BUTTER

Crumpets should be toasted until both sides are crispy and a dark golden colour. They should be eaten piping hot, so whenever possible toast them over an open fire then immediately spread with lashings of butter. Further toppings can be jam, honey, gentleman's relish, cream cheese or Marmite, and they are also absolutely yummy with a poached egg on top.

MUFFINS

These are delicious for breakfast or tea. They should be toasted whole so that the doughy middle stays soft but becomes steaming hot. When the outside is crispy and brown, pull the two halves apart and spread liberally with butter. Try them with jam, honey, marmalade, cheese, Marmite or Gentleman's Relish or with cream cheese and blackcurrant jam.

DOUGHNUTS

*Bennett and Caruthers have vivid memories of the occasion when doughnuts
proved their value as more than just a tea-time indulgence. The two had
strolled casually into town to purchase a bag of the afore-mentioned sugary
items, and were just emerging from the shop when they found themselves caught
up in the middle of a robbery at the jeweller's store next door. Two villains
came rushing out of the shop just in front of the lads, and would have made a
successful escape had not Bennett had the presence of mind to start running after
them – hurling doughnuts at them as he ran. Two well-aimed sticky spheroids
did the trick: the scoundrels were caught, and Bennett and Caruthers were the
heroes of the day.*

•

PREPARATION 2½ HOURS, COOKING 15–20 MINUTES

8 oz/225 g plain flour
¼ teaspoon salt
¾ oz/20 g lard, softened
1 oz/25 g margarine, softened
1 oz/25 g fresh yeast
1 oz/25 g caster sugar
¼ pint/600 ml warm milk
1 medium egg, beaten
Oil for deep-frying
1 tablespoon ground
Cinnamon mixed with 1 tablespoon caster sugar

1   Pre-heat the oven to Gas 1/140°C/275°F. Mix together the flour
and salt and warm them in an ovenproof bowl for 10–15 minutes.

2   Rub the lard and margarine into the flour until the mixture
resembles fine breadcrumbs. Cream the yeast with 1 teaspoon of the sugar
and blend thoroughly. Mix in the rest of the sugar, then the milk and
beaten egg.

3   Make a well in the middle of the flour. Pour in the milk and yeast
mixture and, using a fork, gradually mix in the flour. Leave the dough in
the bowl and stand it in a warm place for 1½–2 hours to rise.

4   Turn the dough out onto a floured board and knead lightly for a few
minutes, then roll out to a thickness of ½ in/1 cm. Cut into rings, using a
2½-in/6-cm cutter dipped in flour, and then cut out the middles using a
1½-in/4-cm cutter. Place the rings on a floured board and leave in a
warm place to rise for 5–10 minutes.

5   Heat a saucepan or deep-fryer half full of oil until it is very hot and
faintly smoking. Using a slotted spoon, drop 3–4 doughnuts carefully
into the oil and cook for 4–5 minutes. Lift out, drain well on paper towel
and then toss in the cinnamon sugar. Keep warm and repeat until all the
doughnuts are cooked.

ECCLES CAKES

PREPARATION 20–25 MINUTES PLUS 2 HOURS FOR THE PASTRY IF USING HOME MADE.
COOKING 10–15 MINUTES
MAKES 2 CAKES

6 oz/175 g flaky pastry, frozen and thawed – or home made (see below)
Flour for rolling
1 oz/25 g butter, softened
1 oz/25 g soft brown sugar
1 oz/25 g mixed candied peel
3 oz/75 g currants
1 medium egg white, beaten
2 tablespoons caster sugar

To make flaky pastry
4 oz/100 g plain flour, sifted
½ teaspoon salt
3 oz/75 g butter or 1½ oz/40 g butter and 1½ oz/40 g lard
Few drops of lemon juice
2–3 fl oz/55–75 ml cold water

1   Mix together the flour and salt. Divide the fat into 4 portions. Rub one portion into the flour. Mix in the lemon juice and enough cold water to bind together to a soft dough similar in consistency to butter. Knead lightly on a floured board until really smooth.

2   Roll out the dough to a rectangle 3 times longer than it is wide. Use the second portion of fat to dot the top two-thirds of the dough. Fold up the bottom one-third and fold down the top one-third. Seal the edges with the rolling pin. Wrap in a plastic bag and chill for 15 minutes.

3   Place the dough on a floured board with the folded edges to your left and right. Roll out into a long strip again and repeat the dotting with the third portion of fat, folding and chilling again. Repeat the whole process once more. Wrap again and chill for 45 minutes–1 hour.

4   Roll out the pastry on a floured board. Cut out 12 circles using a 4-in/10-cm cutter dipped in flour.

5   Cream together the butter and sugar until light and fluffy. Mix in the peel and currants. Place teaspoons of the mixture in the middle of each circle of pastry. Dampen the edges of the pastry with water and close them up over the middle. Turn them over so that the join is underneath.

6   Grease 2 baking trays with a little butter. On a floured board roll out each filled ball of pastry to a thickness of about ⅜ in/1 cm so that the currants just show. Place on the prepared trays and chill for 10–15 minutes. Meanwhile heat the oven to Gas 8/230°C/450°F.

7   Make 3 slits across the top of each cake, brush all over with the beaten egg white and dredge with caster sugar. Bake for 10–15 minutes.

FRUIT CAKE

PREPARATION 15 MINUTES, COOKING 3 HOURS

6 oz/175 g plain flour
Pinch of salt
1 level teaspoon baking powder
1 level teaspoon mixed spice
4 oz/100 g butter
4 oz/100 g soft brown sugar
1½ oz/40 g golden syrup
2 eggs, beaten
11 oz/325 g mixed fruit (raisins, currants, sultanas, glacé cherries)
2 oz/50 g candied peel
2½ fl oz/60 ml milk

1   Pre-heat the oven to Gas 4/180°C/350°F. Line and grease a 7-in/18-cm round cake tin.

2   Mix together the flour, salt, baking powder and spice. Cream together the butter, sugar and syrup until light and fluffy. Add the eggs a little at a time, alternating with the flour mixture. Beat well after each addition.

3   Add the dried fruit and milk and mix thoroughly to a fairly soft consistency. Pour into the cake tin and bake in the middle of the oven for 30 minutes, then turn the oven down to Gas 2/150°C/310°F and bake for a further 2–2½ hours.

4   Test with a skewer. If the skewer comes out clean the cake is ready. Remove from the oven and leave to cool in the tin for 20–30 minutes. Turn out onto a wire rack and leave to cool completely.

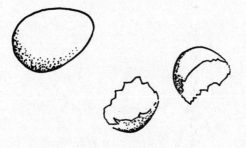

STICKY GINGERBREAD

PREPARATION 10 MINUTES, COOKING 1 HOUR

2 oz/50 g margarine
2 oz/50 g lard
4 generous tablespoons golden syrup
2 oz/50 g demerara sugar
9 oz/250 g self-raising flour
2 oz/50 g chopped crystallized ginger
Pinch of salt
2 teaspoons ground ginger
1 teaspoon mixed spice
¼ pint/150 ml warm milk
½ teaspoon bicarbonate of soda

1   Pre-heat the oven to Gas 3/170°C/325°F and line and grease a 7-in/ 18-cm round tin or a 2-lb/900-g loaf tin.

2   Melt the fats together in a medium-sized saucepan. Add the syrup and sugar and melt, but do not really heat. Add the dry ingredients and fruit and mix thoroughly.

3   Dissolve the bicarbonate of soda in the warm milk and add to the cake mixture. Stir in carefully. Pour into the prepared tin and bake for 1 hour. Remove from the oven and leave to cool in the tin for about 30 minutes. Turn out onto a wire rack and leave to cool completely.

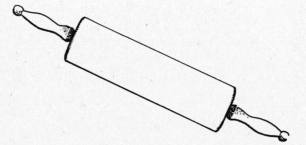

MINCE PIES

PREPARATION 25–30 MINUTES, INCLUDING TIME TO CHILL THE PASTRY,
COOKING 25–30 MINUTES
MAKES 8–10

6 oz/100 g rich shortcrust pastry (see page 45)
12 oz/350 g mincemeat
Caster sugar for sprinkling

1　Pre-heat the oven to Gas 5/190°C/375°F, and grease 8–10 patty tins.

2　Make the pastry as for jam tarts and roll out to about ⅛ in/3 mm. Cut half the pastry into rounds using a 2½-in/6-cm cutter dipped in flour. These rounds will form the lids.

3　Cut the remaining pastry into rounds using a 3-in/7.5-cm cutter dipped in flour, and use to line the patty tins. Spoon the mincemeat into the middle of each. Brush the edges of the pastry with water and place a lid on top of each. Press the edges well together. Brush the tops with water and sprinkle lightly with caster sugar.

4　Make a hole or two small cuts in the top of each and bake for 25–30 minutes until lightly golden. Remove from the oven and sprinkle with more sugar. Serve hot or cold.

PARKIN

Our five friends always enjoy Parkin because, being a Bonfire Night treat, they are reminded of the fun and excitment of fireworks parties.

●

PREPARATION 5–10 MINUTES, COOKING 2 HOURS
MAKES 18–20 PIECES

1½ lb/675 g medium oatmeal
8 oz/225 g soft brown sugar
1½ teaspoon ground ginger
1½ teaspoon allspice or mixed spice
1 lb/450 g treacle
8 oz/225 g butter

1　Pre-heat the oven to Gas 3/170°C/325°F and grease a shallow baking tin about 12 × 9 in/30 × 23 cm.

2　Place the oatmeal in a bowl and mix in the sugar, ginger and spice.

3　Warm the treacle and butter together in a small pan until the butter has melted. Stir into the oatmeal mixture and mix thoroughly. Pour into the prepared tin and bake for about 2 hours till the cake is firm and springs back when pressed with a finger.

LARDY CAKE

PREPARATION 1½–2 HOURS, COOKING 30 MINUTES
MAKES 9 PIECES

½ oz/15 g fresh yeast
1 tablespoon caster sugar
½ pint/300 ml warm water
1 lb/450 g plain flour, sifted
2 teaspoons salt
2 tablespoon oil to grease the bowl and tin
14 oz/400 g lard, softened
6 oz/175 g granulated sugar
¼ teaspoon nutmeg, cinnamon or allspice
2 oz/50 g sultanas or raisins
2 oz/50 g sugar cubes, crushed

1   Cream together the yeast, caster sugar and water. Mix the flour and salt together in a bowl and make a well in the middle. Pour in the yeast mixture and gradually mix to a soft dough, using a fork.

2   Turn onto a floured board and knead for about 5 minutes until smooth and elastic. Wash, dry and lightly oil the bowl, replace the dough in it and cover with a damp cloth. Leave in a warm place for 1–1½ hours until doubled in size.

3   Pre-heat the oven to Gas 6/200°C/400°F and oil an 8-in/20-cm square cake tin. Turn the dough onto a floured board and knead again for 5 minutes. Roll out into a rectangle about ½-in/1-cm thick. Dot the surface with a third of the lard and sprinkle with a third of the granulated sugar. Fold the bottom third of the dough up, and the top third down over it. Turn the dough so that the folded sides are on your left and right.

4   Roll out again to a rectangle. Dot the surface with another third of the lard and sprinkle with another third of the sugar. Repeat the folding, rolling, dotting and sprinkling once more. On the last dotting and sprinkling, also sprinkle over the spices, diced fruit and crushed cube sugar. Fold and roll to a square to fit the tin.

5   Place the dough in the tin and mark into 9 squares. Bake for 30 minutes until pale golden. Remove from the oven and turn out onto a wire rack to cool. When cool, break (don't cut) into pieces.

JAM TARTS

PREPARATION 25–30 MINUTES, INCLUDING TIME TO CHILL THE PASTRY,
COOKING 20–25 MINUTES
MAKES 12–14

For the rich shortcrust pastry
6 oz/175 g plain flour, sifted
Pinch of salt
4½ oz/115 g butter, softened
1 egg yolk
1½ teaspoons caster sugar
About 1 tablespoon cold water

For the tarts
12 oz/350 ml jam of your choice

1   To make the pastry, mix together the flour and salt. Rub in the butter until the mixture resembles fine breadcrumbs. Make a well in the middle and put in the egg yolk. Sprinkle the sugar over. With the knife gradually mix the egg into the flour. Mix in enough water, a little at a time, to form a stiff but pliable dough, then knead lightly. Wrap in a plastic bag and chill in the refrigerator for at least 15 minutes.

2   Heat the oven to Gas 5/190°C/375°F. Roll out the pastry on a floured board to a thickness of about ⅛ in/3 mm. Cut into rounds using a 3-in/7.5-cm cutter dipped in flour.

3   Grease 12–14 patty tins and line with the pastry circles. Spoon some jam into the middle of each – not too much or it will boil over and burn while the tarts are cooking. Bake for 20–25 minutes. Serve hot or cold.

◇4◇

After
The Match
There Was Tea
On The Lawn

THE morning of the cricket match at Westcombe Manor dawned bright and warm. The County Team was to play Westcombe Village and the Major had telephoned the Caruthers' residence to see if Caruthers' father would be available to take his place in the team. Caruthers had explained the situation and had suggested that, should the Major be short of a man, Patterson might be of some service. He was, after all, school cricket captain, a capital bowler and jolly useful with a bat. The Major had expressed his delight and had at once recruited Patterson for the team. The chums were absolutely thrilled.

When they arrived at the Manor the first spectators were just settling in. The ground was in splendid order and at 11 o'clock two of the county men took their places at the wickets, the umpires gave the signal and the

ESSENTIAL SUPPLIES WERE DROPPED
TO THE BRITISH AGENTS....

match began. Presently the batsmen began to warm to their work and made one or two good hits. Then Patterson, who was bowling at one end, took the middle stump. The village contingent cheered lustily. 'Well bowled, Patterson! Well bowled!' The match passed off without further excitement. There was some first-rate batting and some good sound bowling. The county team won by two wickets after a closer match than anticipated. The Major's team was comforted by feeling quite sure that they had played their best and had been admirably supported by their guest player. As they strolled up to the Manor for tea, the Major clapped Patterson on the back. 'Jolly good show, my lad! By Jove, that bit of bowling at the start certainly set the tone of the match. Be happy to have you in my team any time!'

SANDWICHES

BANANA AND GRATED CHOCOLATE

PREPARATION 5 MINUTES
MAKES 4 ROUNDS

4 bananas
4 oz/100 g plain chocolate

Grate the chocolate and sprinkle over 4 slices of buttered bread. Slice the banana and lay carefully over the chocolate. Press the other slices of buttered bread on top and cut into squares and triangles. Eat immediately, as the banana will go brown if left for too long.

BLUE CHEESE AND WATERCRESS

PREPARATION 5 MINUTES
MAKES 4 ROUNDS

7–8 oz/200 g–225 g blue cheese such as dolcelatte, Roquefort or creamy
Stilton
15–20 sprigs of watercress, washed carefully
A little mayonnaise

Spread mayonnaise sparingly on 4 slices of buttered or unbuttered bread. Cover with a generous layer of cheese, then lay the sprigs of watercress on top. Press the other slices of bread on top. Trim off the crusts and cut into squares or triangles.

CHEESE, LETTUCE AND WALNUT

PREPARATION 5 MINUTES
MAKES 4 ROUNDS

4 oz/100 g chopped walnuts
8 oz/225 g mature Cheddar, grated
A few crisp lettuce leaves, washed, dried and shredded
Salt and freshly ground black pepper

Mix together the walnuts and cheese. Spread the mixture over 4 slices of buttered bread, and carefully lay the shredded lettuce over the top. Season with salt and pepper. Press the other slices of buttered bread on top and cut into squares or triangles.

CHICKEN MAYONNAISE

PREPARATION 5 MINUTES
MAKES 4 ROUNDS

**8 oz/225 g cold cooked chicken
2 tablespoons chopped fresh chives
1½ tablespoon mayonnaise
Salt and freshly ground black pepper
2 punnets mustard and cress**

Mix the chicken, chives and mayonnaise together and season with salt and pepper. Pile the mixture on to 4 slices of buttered or unbuttered bread and place a generous portion of mustard and cress on top. Press the other 4 slices of bread on top. Trim off the crusts and cut into squares or triangles.

CREAM CHEESE AND
BLACKCURRANT JAM

PREPARATION 3 MINUTES
MAKES 4 ROUNDS

**6 oz/175 g cream cheese, softened
2–3 tablespoons blackcurrant jam**

Spread 4 slices of bread with the cream cheese, buttering first if liked. Cover with a layer of jam, then press the other 4 slices of bread on top. Trim off the crusts and cut into squares, triangles or fingers.

CREAM CHEESE AND SMOKED SALMON

PREPARATION 5 MINUTES
MAKES 4 ROUNDS

**6 oz/175 g cream cheese, softened
10–11 oz/275–325 g sliced smoked salmon
2 teaspoons freshly squeezed lemon juice
Freshly ground black pepper**

Butter 8 slices of wholewheat bread or leave unbuttered. Spread 4 slices with the cream cheese and lay the salmon on top. Sprinkle with lemon juice and a generous grinding of black pepper. Press the remaining slices of bread on top, trim off the crusts and cut into triangles.

CUCUMBER

PREPARATION 10 MINUTES
MAKES 4 ROUNDS

½ cucumber, peeled and thinly sliced
2 teaspoons freshly squeezed lemon juice
Salt and freshly ground black pepper

Place the slices of cucumber in a bowl with the lemon juice, salt and pepper, and turn carefully so that all the slices are coated. Leave for 2–3 minutes. Butter 8 slices of bread, and lay the cucumber on 4 of them. Carefully press the 4 remaining slices of bread on top, trim off the crusts and cut into squares or triangles.

EGG MAYONNAISE AND CRESS

PREPARATION 15 MINUTES
MAKES 4 ROUNDS

4 medium eggs
2 tablespoons mayonnaise
Salt and freshly ground black pepper
2 punnets of mustard and cress

Boil the eggs for 6–8 minutes. Drain and immediately run under cold water. Shell the eggs and mash thoroughly. Add the mayonnaise, salt and pepper and mix well together. Butter 8 slices of bread or leave unbuttered and spread the mixture onto 4 of them. Scatter some mustard and cress over the egg, then press the remaining bread on top. Trim off the crusts and cut into squares or triangles.

PRINCESS

PREPARATION 10 MINUTES
MAKES 4 ROUNDS

2 teaspoons sunflower oil
Dash of cider or tarragon vinegar
Pinch of mild curry powder
Salt and freshly ground black pepper
5 oz/150 g cold cooked chicken, chopped into small pieces
3 oz/75 g cold cooked ham or tongue, chopped
½ oz/15 g mature Cheddar, grated
2 hard-boiled egg yolks

Mix together the oil, vinegar, curry powder, salt and pepper, then add the meats, cheese and egg yolks. Mix thoroughly. Butter 8 slices of bread or leave unbuttered, and pile the mixture onto 4 of them, pressing the remainder. Trim off the crusts and cut into triangles or squares.

SARDINE AND TOMATO

PREPARATION 5 MINUTES
MAKES 4 ROUNDS

2 × 4.37-oz/124-g cans of sardines in oil
Few drops of freshly squeezed lemon juice
4–5 firm tomatoes, thinly sliced
Salt and freshly ground black pepper

Drain the oil from the sardines, remove the bones and mash the flesh with the lemon juice. Butter 8 slices of bread and spread the mixture onto 4 of them, topping with the tomato slices. Season with salt and pepper, press the remaining slices of bread on top and cut into squares or triangles.

POTTED SHRIMPS

PREPARATION AND COOKING 1½ HOURS
MAKES 4 HELPINGS

8 oz/225 g fresh peeled shrimps
¼ teaspoon ground mace
¼ teaspoon ground cloves
Pinch of ground nutmeg
Salt and freshly ground black pepper
6 oz/175 g butter

1   Pre-heat the oven to Gas 2/150°C/310°F.

2   Place the shrimps in a shallow baking dish and sprinkle over the spices, salt and pepper. Melt 2 oz/50 g of the butter and pour over the shrimps. Bake for 10–15 minutes.

3   Remove from the oven. Stir well and divide the shrimps between 4 ramekins or individual dishes. Chill for 30 minutes in the refrigerator.

4   Clarify the remaining butter by heating slowly in a small pan, removing the scum as it rises. When the butter is quite clear, pour over the shrimps and leave for ½–¾ hour to set in the refrigerator. Serve with slices of brown buttered toast.

Ham Pâté on Toast

PREPARATION 10 MINUTES
MAKES ENOUGH FOR 4 SLICES

½ oz/15 g butter
1 finely chopped shallot
6 oz/175 g finely chopped cooked ham
2 egg yolks
1 tablespoon double cream
Freshly ground black pepper
½ teaspoon finely chopped parsley
Slices of buttered toast with crusts removed

1   Melt the butter in a small pan and gently fry the shallot until golden brown. Add the ham and stir until heated through.

2   Add the egg yolks, cream and pepper to taste, and stir over a moderate heat until the mixture thickens. Leave to cool.

3   Spread onto the buttered toast, sprinkle with parsley and cut into fingers.

Cheese Straws

PREPARATION 10 MINUTES, COOKING 15–20 MINUTES
MAKES ABOUT 20 STRAWS

3 oz/75 g plain flour
2 oz/50 g butter, softened
2 oz/50 g grated Parmesan
Cayenne pepper
Salt and freshly ground black pepper
1 egg yolk

1   Pre-heat the oven to Gas 3/170°C/325°F and grease a baking tray.

2   Place the flour in a bowl and rub in the butter. Add the cheese, a good pinch of cayenne, salt and pepper.

3   Add the egg yolk and mix all the ingredients together to form a stiff paste. Roll it out on a floured board to a thickness of ½ in/1 cm. Cut into strips about 2 in/5 cm long.

4   Bake on the prepared baking tray for 15–20 minutes till lightly golden. Remove from the oven and leave to cool.

BATTENBURG CAKE

PREPARATION AND COOKING 2–2¼ HOURS

8 oz/225 g butter or margarine
8 oz/225 g caster sugar plus extra for dusting
4 eggs, well beaten
8 oz/225 g plain flour
Pinch of salt
3 level teaspoons baking powder
Pink food colouring
1–2 tablespoons (15.30 ml) apricot jam
4 oz/100 g marzipan

1   Make 2 Victoria sponge cakes as follows. Pre-heat the oven to Gas 4/180°C/350°F and grease 2 × 2-lb/900-g loaf tins approximately 9 × 4 × 2½ in/23 × 10 × 6 cm.

2   Cream 4 oz/100 g butter or margarine with 4 oz/100 g caster sugar and beat until light and fluffy. Gradually add half the beaten egg, beating thoroughly after each addition.

3   Sift together the flour, salt and baking powder and fold carefully into the mixture. Mix to a soft dropping consistency by adding a little warm water if necessary.

4   Pour the mixture into one of the prepared tins and bake for 40–50 minutes.

5   Repeat the process for the second cake but add a few drops of pink food colouring.

6   Remove the cakes from the oven and leave to cool in the tin for 10–15 minutes. Then turn out onto a wire rack and leave to cool completely.

7   Cut the cakes into strips 8–9 in/20–23 cm long and 1½ in/4 cm square. Two pink strips and two white strips will be needed. Join the strips together with the apricot jam to make a block 9 × 3 × 3 in/23 × 7.5 × 7.5 cm with a pink and white strip side by side, topped by a white and pink strip side by side.

8   Roll the marzipan into an oblong wide enough and long enough to wrap around the cake, leaving the ends open. Trim the edges. Spread the top of the cake with apricot jam and invert onto the marzipan.

9   Spread the remaining three sides of the cake with apricot jam. Roll up inside the marzipan and join the edges of the marzipan by pinching carefully together. Dust with caster sugar.

CHOCOLATE CAKE

PREPARATION AND COOKING 1¼–1½ HOURS

4 oz/100 g plain chocolate
5 oz/150 g margarine or butter, softened
5 oz/150 g caster sugar
3 eggs, beaten
1 tablespoon milk
8 oz/225 g self-raising flour, sifted
Pinch of salt
A few chocolate buttons, optional

For the icing
1½ oz/50 g butter, softened
4 oz/100 g icing sugar
2 teaspoons milk
1 tablespoon cocoa
1 tablespoon hot water

1   Pre-heat the oven to Gas 4/180°C/350°F and grease and line a 7-in/ 18-cm round cake tin.

2   Melt the chocolate in a bowl over hot water. Cream together the fat and sugar until light and fluffy. Beat in the eggs one at a time.

3   Stir the milk into the melted chocolate and add to the creamed mixture. Fold in the flour and salt. Pour into the prepared tin and bake for 1 hour 10 minutes or until firm. Remove from the oven and leave to cool in the tin for 10–15 minutes, then turn out onto a wire rack and leave to cool completely.

4   To make the icing, mix the cocoa with the hot water. Beat together the butter and the icing sugar. Add the other ingredients and beat well. Ice the cake when cool, and decorate by drawing the prongs of a fork through the icing to make a pattern. If liked, place a few chocolate buttons around the edge of the cake.

MACAROONS

PREPARATION 10–15 MINUTES, COOKING 20–30 MINUTES
MAKES 20

Rice paper
2 egg whites
4 oz/100 g caster sugar
3 oz/75 g ground almonds
1 teaspoon rice flour
½ teaspoon vanilla essence
Whole blanched almonds to decorate

1   Pre-heat the oven to Gas 4/180°C/350°F and place sheets of rice paper ready on baking trays.

2   Beat the egg whites stiffly in a large bowl. Mix the sugar, ground almonds and rice flour together and fold into the egg whites. Add the vanilla essence.

3   Place the mixture in a large piping bag with a ½-in/1-cm plain nozzle. Pipe onto the rice paper in rounds about 1½ in/4 cm in diameter. Place an almond in the centre of each and bake for 20–30 minutes until lightly golden. Remove from the oven and leave to cool.

Note: Rice flour and rice paper can be obtained from most health-food shops.

SHORTBREAD

PREPARATION 10 MINUTES, COOKING 35 MINUTES
MAKES 12 PIECES

4 oz/100 g margarine or butter
2 oz/50 g caster sugar, plus extra for sprinkling
4 oz/100 g plain flour, sifted
2 oz/50 g cornflour, sifted
Grated rind of 1 orange

1   Pre-heat the oven to Gas 3/170°C/325°F and grease a 7-in/18-cm square cake tin.

2   Cream the fat and sugar together until light and fluffy. Add the other ingredients, mix thoroughly and knead lightly for 2–3 minutes.

3   Press into the prepared tin and smooth the top with a palette knife. Prick with a fork and sprinkle lightly with caster sugar. Place in the refrigerator for 15 minutes.

4   Bake for 35 minutes until lightly golden. Remove from the oven and leave to cool in the tin for 5 minutes. Cut carefully into 12 pieces while still warm.

BRANDY SNAPS

PREPARATION AND COOKING 30–35 MINUTES
MAKES 12–16

1 oz/25 g butter or margarine
2½ oz/65 g caster sugar
1 oz/25 g golden syrup
1 oz/25 g plain flour, sifted
1 teaspoon ground ginger
1 pint/600 ml double cream, whipped

1   Pre-heat the oven to Gas 2/150°C/310°F and grease 2 baking trays.

2   Cream the fat, sugar and syrup together till light and fluffy. Stir in the flour and ginger. Form into 12–16 balls and place well apart on the prepared baking trays. Bake until a rich brown colour (about 10–15 minutes).

3   Remove from the oven and allow to cool slightly. Remove from the baking tray with a knife and, while still warm and soft enough, roll round handles of wooden spoons. Leave until set, then slide carefully off.

4   Add a little caster sugar to the whipped cream, if liked, and pipe into the brandy snaps. Eat immediately.

SWISS ROLL

PREPARATION 15 MINUTES, COOKING 7–10 MINUTES

3 medium eggs
4 oz/100 g caster sugar
3 oz/75 g plain flour, sifted
1 tablespoon hot water
3 tablespoons jam of choice

1   Pre-heat the oven to Gas 6 200°C/400°F and grease and line an 11 × 7 in/28 × 18 cm Swiss roll tin.

2   Beat the eggs and sugar together in a bowl set over a saucepan of simmering water until the mixture leaves a trail when the beater is lifted. This will take 7–8 minutes. Fold in the flour and hot water.

3   Pour into the prepared tin and bake for 8–10 minutes until lightly golden and firm. Have ready a sheet of greaseproof paper. Place it on top of a damp cloth and sprinkle with about 2 tablespoons of caster sugar. Remove the cake from the oven and turn immediately onto the sugared paper. Peel off the lining paper.

4   While still hot, trim the edges of the cake and spread with the jam. Roll the cake up, hold in place for a few minutes, then transfer to a wire rack to cool. Before serving dredge with 2 tablespoons caster sugar.

DUNDEE CAKE

PREPARATION 15 MINUTES, COOKING 2½–3 HOURS

8 oz/225 g butter, softened
8 oz/225 g caster sugar
Grated rind of 1 large orange
4 medium eggs, beaten
8 oz/225 g plain flour, softened
2 oz/50 g ground almonds
1 oz/25 g mixed candied peel
4 oz/100 g currants
4 oz/100 g sultanas
4 oz/100 g raisins
2 oz/50 g glacé cherries, quartered
40–50 split almonds

1   Pre-heat the oven to Gas 2/150°C/310°F and grease and line a 7-in/ 18-cm round cake tin.

2   Cream the butter and sugar together until light and fluffy. Beat in the orange rind and the eggs, one at a time, adding 1 tablespoon of the flour with each egg. Beat thoroughly.

3   With a metal spoon, stir in the ground almonds and dried fruit. Fold in the remaining flour. Turn the mixture into the prepared tin and arrange the split almonds over the whole of the top.

4   Bake for 2½–3 hours until a skewer comes out clean. Remove from the oven and leave in the tin for 2–3 minutes, then turn out onto a wire rack to cool completely.

DROP SCONES

PREPARATION AND COOKING 50–55 MINUTES
MAKES 18–20

**8 oz/225 g self-raising flour, sifted
Pinch of salt
1 teaspoon cream of tartar
½ teaspoon bicarbonate of soda
1 oz/25 g caster sugar
1 large egg, beaten
8 fl oz/225 ml warm milk
Oil or lard to grease the griddle**

1   Mix together all the dry ingredients. Make a well in the middle and pour the eggs into it. Mix the eggs gradually into the flour with a wooden spoon, working the flour down from the sides. Very gradually add the milk and continue mixing until all the flour has been mixed in. Beat hard for 2–3 minutes.

2   Leave the batter to stand for 10 minutes. Meanwhile warm the griddle (or heavy frying pan) and brush with melted lard or oil. Regulate the heat so that the griddle reaches an even all-over temperature.

3   Drop spoonfuls of the batter onto the griddle and leave to cook slowly until bubbles appear and break. After about 4 minutes turn the scones very carefully and cook for a further 3–4 minutes until the underside is golden. Remove from the griddle, brush more lard or oil onto the hot surface and repeat until all the batter is cooked.
The scones are best eaten hot with lashings of butter, and either honey, jam or lemon curd.

VICTORIA SPONGE

PREPARATION 10 MINUTES, COOKING 20–25 MINUTES

4 oz/100 g margarine or butter, softened
4 oz/100 g caster sugar
2 medium eggs, beaten
4 oz/100 g self-raising flour, sifted
1 tablespoon boiling water
2–3 oz/50–75 g raspberry jam

1   Pre-heat the oven to Gas 4 180°C/350°F and line and grease 2 × 7-in/18-cm round sandwich tins.

2   Cream the fat and sugar together until light and fluffy. Beat in the eggs a little at a time, adding 1 tablespoon of the flour between additions. Beat thoroughly. Fold in the remaining flour with a metal spoon. Finally, stir in the boiling water and mix well.

3   Divide the mixture between the prepared tins and bake for 25–30 minutes until the cake is lightly browned and springs back when pressed lightly with a finger.

4   Remove from the oven and turn out onto a wire rack to cool. When cold spread the underside of one cake with the jam, lay the other cake on top and dredge with caster sugar.

Other fillings:

These fillings are also delicious! Try whipped cream with the jam; or fresh raspberries or strawberries with whipped cream; or vanilla or chocolate butter filling, made with 1½ oz/40 g butter, 4 oz/100 g icing sugar and 1 tablespoon cocoa or a few drops of vanilla essence.

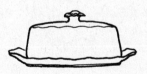

RED FRUIT JELLY

This is rather more exciting than ordinary jelly, and our five cricket fans were very impressed when the Major's wife served it for tea after the exciting match.

•

PREPARATION 25–30 MINUTES (PLUS 2 HOURS TO SET)
MAKES 8 HELPINGS

8 oz/225 g granulated sugar
1½ pints/900 ml water
8 oz/225 g redcurrants
1 lemon
9 teaspoons or 3 envelopes of gelatine
8 oz/225 g raspberries
6 oz/175 g red cherries, with stones removed
2 peaches, peeled and sliced

1   Dissolve the sugar slowly in the water over a low heat, stirring from time to time. Place the redcurrants in the syrup and cook gently for 10–15 minutes. Leave to cool in the syrup.

2   Grate and squeeze the lemon. Measure the lemon juice and make up to 5 tablespoons with water. Place the gelatine in a small pan with the juice and water. Leave until the gelatine has swollen, then add a further 5 tablespoons of water and heat the pan very gently until the gelatine has dissolved.

3   Stir the dissolved gelatine into the redcurrants in the syrup, then add the raspberries, grated lemon rind, the cherries and peaches.

4   Turn into a wet 3½–4 pint/2–2.25 litre mould or glass fruit dish, and leave to set.

LEMONADE

6 lemons
1 oz/25 g demerara sugar or honey
2 pints/1 litre boiling water

1   Slice off the rind of 2 lemons very thinly, with no white pith, then place in a large jug.

2   Peel the other 4 lemons so that all the skin and pith is removed. Slice the flesh thinly, removing all the pips. Add the sugar or honey and the water. Cover and leave until completely cold, then strain.

3   Serve in glasses containing ice cubes and fresh slices of lemon.

ICED TEA

Use Ceylon Breakfast tea for this as it has the property of remaining quite clear when cold – unlike other teas.

Make a pot of tea, adding one extra spoonful of leaves than you would normally. Place a little sugar in a large jug and fill with ice cubes. Strain the tea over the ice cubes and top up with cold water. Chill for several hours. To serve, pour into glasses and garnish with slices of lemon and a few bruised mint or sage leaves.

SUMMER
SENSATIONAL SUNDAE

PREPARATION 15–20 MINUTES
MAKES 4 HELPINGS

For the sauce
8 oz/225 g strawberries
Juice of 1 lemon
3 oz/75 g caster sugar

For the sundae
1 pint/600 ml vanilla or raspberry ripple ice-cream
8 oz/225 g strawberries
8 oz/225 g raspberries
8 small meringue shells
1 pint/600 ml double cream, whipped

1   Divide the strawberries into two equal portions, the first half for the sauce. Hull and wash the strawberries, then place in a blender with the juice of 1 lemon and 3 oz/75 g of caster sugar. Blend thoroughly.

2   Take 4 tall sundae glasses and place in each a small scoop of ice-cream. Reserve 4 strawberries and 4 raspberries for decoration, and place the rest on top of the ice-cream.

3   Lightly crush the meringue shells and sprinkle over the fruit. Put the whipped cream into a piping bag with a large star nozzle and pipe some over. Add a further layer of ice-cream, then more cream. Spoon the strawberry sauce over. Pipe a rosette of cream on top and decorate with 1 strawberry and 1 raspberry. Serve immediately.

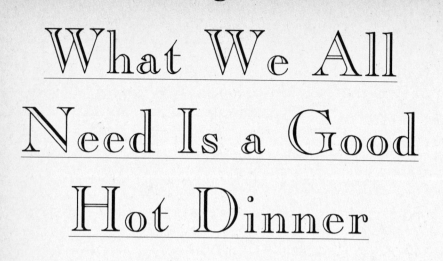

5

What We All Need Is a Good Hot Dinner

THE boat was ready. Everything was in splendid working order and Caruthers telephoned to Kerry's Creek to inform the Captain of their projected visit. The weather was first-rate – clear skies, a light breeze and no chance of rain. They set off and made good progress, but were only about half way to Kerry's Creek when Morrell noticed with some alarm that clouds were looming up behind them. The strengthening wind prepared them for the worst and very soon the storm was upon them. The river quickly became very choppy, slowing their progress, but they battled on against the wind.

As they rounded the bend in the river their attention was caught by distant cries for help. The shouts seemed to come from up ahead. They could just make out a small figure clinging desperately to an overhanging tree. 'Hang on, old chap,' they shouted as they drew slowly closer to the unfortunate lad. 'We'll have you down from there in no time!' Caruthers and Bennett held firmly to the low branches while the lad was lifted to safety. He was white-faced, cold and extremely wet.

As the boat struggled up the last stretch of river, Captain Bates was already on the jetty, watching out for them. He had become concerned at the lateness of their arrival in such appalling conditions, and as they clambered from the boat they explained the delay. They discussed the mishap and chatted happily about their other adventures since last visiting the Captain. Later, after the boy had been collected by his father, their host said, 'Well now – it's much too wet and much too late for you to set off back today. You must spend the night here and we'll hope for better weather tomorrow. What we all need is a good hot dinner!'

IT WAS HUNGARIAN COOKING
ALLRIGHT.....

BACON ROLL

The lads and their schoolfellows usually enjoy Cook's Bacon Roll, but since a rather unfortunate occurrence they are somewhat wary of it. They were just tucking into generous portions of the roll one day, when Morrell gave a loud exclamation of horror. 'Good Lord' he uttered, 'whatever is that in my dinner?' 'By jove' said Caruthers, 'it looks exactly like a set of false teeth.' Indeed, that is just what it was, although how it had made its way into the bacon roll they could not fathom. Cook understandably denied all knowledge of the matter, and to this day the pals do not know the cause of the surprise in Morrell's dinner!

•

PREPARATION AND COOKING 1¾ HOURS
MAKES 5–6 HELPINGS

8 oz/225 g streaky bacon
1 medium onion, peeled and roughly chopped
Salt and freshly ground black pepper
12 oz/350 g self-raising flour
6 oz/175 g shredded suet
Cold water
Parsley to garnish

For the sauce
1 × 14-oz/400-g can chopped tomatoes
1 teaspoon demerara sugar
1 teaspoon Worcester sauce
Salt and freshly ground black pepper
Pinch of dried sage
Few drops of freshly squeezed lemon juice

1   Pre-heat the oven to Gas 6/200°C/400°F and grease a baking tray.

2   Remove rind and any bone from the bacon, cut it into small pieces and mix with the chopped onion and seasoning.

3   Mix together the flour and suet and add enough cold water to mix to a soft but not sticky dough. Turn onto a floured board and knead lightly, then roll out to about ½ in/1 cm thick. Place the bacon mixture on it to within 1 in/2.5 cm of the edges. Brush the edges with water and roll up. Seal the ends carefully and wrap the entire roll loosely in foil.

4   Place on the prepared baking tray and bake in the centre of the oven for 1½ hours until golden brown.

5   To make the sauce place the tomatoes, sugar, Worcester sauce, seasoning, sage and lemon juice in a pan. Bring slowly to the boil and simmer gently for about 45 minutes.

6   Place the bacon roll on a warmed serving dish and garnish with parsley. Serve the sauce separately in a gravy boat.

Baked Ham

And Pease Pudding

PREPARATION AND COOKING 2–2¼ HOURS
MAKES 5–6 HELPINGS

A 3-lb/1.35-kg ham, pre-soaked for at least 12 hours
Plain flour
Cloves
Demerara sugar

The pease pudding
1½ pints/900 ml split peas, soaked overnight
½ teaspoon salt
1 small onion, peeled but whole
Small bunch of herbs or bouquet garni
2 oz/50 g butter
2 eggs
Salt and freshly ground black pepper

1   Pre-heat the oven to Gas 6/200°C/400°F.

2   Remove the ham from the water and wipe well. Mix the flour and water together to make a thick paste. Place the ham in a baking dish and coat with the paste, which must be thick enough to keep in the juices.

3   Leave the ham in the oven as set for about 15 minutes, then reduce the heat to Gas 2/150°C/310°F and cook for a further 1½ hours. Remove from the oven and turn the temperature up to Gas 8/230°C/450°F. Break off the crust and the skin. With a sharp knife score even criss-crosses in the fat, place a clove in each square and sprinkle brown sugar over the fat.

4   The pease pudding can be made in advance and heated through or made while the ham is cooking. Remove any discoloured peas; rinse and place in a medium-sized pan. Cover with cold water and add the salt, the onion and the herbs or bouquet garni. Bring to the boil and simmer very gently for 2–2½ hours until tender. Drain well and remove the onion and herbs or bouquet garni.

5   Rub through a sieve or blend in a food processor or blender. Add the butter, the beaten eggs, salt and black pepper to taste. Beat well together. Place inside a floured cloth and tie up tightly.

6   Place in a pan of water. Bring the water to the boil and boil the pudding inside the bag for 1 hour. Turn out and serve immediately.

7   Return the ham to the oven for 5–10 minutes until the sugar melts and forms a glaze over the meat. Remove and serve immediately.

Note: The ham can be served with vegetables instead of pease pudding if preferred, or the pease pudding can be used as an accompaniment to another dish, such as pork sausages.

BEEF OLIVES

PREPARATION AND COOKING 1¾–2 HOURS
MAKES 5–6 HELPINGS

1½ lb/675 g stewing steak, sliced thinly
2 oz/50 g fresh white breadcrumbs
4 tablespoons chopped suet
2 tablespoons chopped fresh parsley
½ teaspoon dried mixed herbs
Grated rind of ½ lemon
Salt and freshly ground black pepper
1 egg, beaten
1 oz/25 g plain flour, seasoned with salt and pepper
2 oz/50 g dripping or butter
8 oz/225 g onions, peeled and sliced
1 pint/600 ml stock

1   Remove any excess fat from the meat and cut it into strips about 1½ × 3 in/4 × 7.5 cm.

2   Mix together the breadcrumbs, suet, parsley, herbs, lemon rind and seasoning. Use enough beaten egg to bind lightly together.

3   Divide this stuffing between the strips of meat and roll each one into a neat roll, tying with string or thread to secure. Roll the beef olives in the seasoned flour.

4   Heat the fat in a medium-sized pan and fry the meat until browned all over. Lift out carefully with a slotted spoon. Fry the onions until transparent, then return the meat to the pan with any remaining flour. Pour in the stock and bring slowly to the boil. Simmer gently, with a lid on the pan, for about 1½ hours until the meat is tender.

IRISH STEW

PREPARATION AND COOKING 2–2¼ HOURS
MAKES 5–6 HELPINGS

2 lb/900 g best end of neck of lamb
1 lb/450 g onions, peeled and thinly sliced
Salt and freshly ground black pepper
3 lb/1.5 kg potatoes, peeled and sliced
1½ pint/900 ml stock or water
Chopped parsley to garnish

1   Cut the meat into neat pieces and trim off any fat. In a large saucepan arrange layers of meat, onions, salt and pepper and potatoes. Add enough stock or water to just cover. Bring to the boil and simmer for about 1¾–2 hours, or until the meat and potatoes are tender.

2   Before serving sprinkle the parsley over the top.

FISH PIE

PREPARATION AND COOKING 1 HOUR
MAKES 5–6 HELPINGS

½ oz/15 g butter
½ oz/15 g plain flour
½ pint/300 ml milk (or fish stock)
1½ lb/675 g cold cooked white fish, flaked
2 hard-boiled eggs, finely chopped
1 tablespoon chopped fresh parsley
1 teaspoon grated lemon rind
Salt and freshly ground black pepper
2–2½ lb/900–1000g potatoes
1 oz/25 g butter

1   First make the white sauce. Melt the butter in a small pan. Add the flour and stir over a moderate heat for 2–3 minutes. Remove from the heat and gradually add the milk or fish stock. Stir thoroughly. Return to the heat and stir until the sauce thickens.

2   In a large bowl mix together the flaked fish, eggs, parsley, lemon rind and sauce. Turn carefully until all the ingredients are evenly distributed.

3   Peel the potatoes and cut into small pieces. Place in a pan with enough cold water to just cover and add 1 teaspoon of salt. Bring to the boil and simmer for 15–20 minutes until tender. Strain and mash carefully.

4   Pre-heat the oven to Gas 4/180°C/350°F. Place the fish mixture in an ovenproof dish, spoon the potato over the top and spread out carefully. Dot with the butter. Cook in the oven for 25–30 minutes until the potato has just browned. Serve immediately.

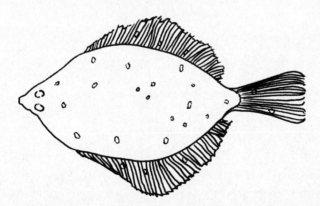

LANCASHIRE HOTPOT

PREPARATION AND COOKING 2¼–2½ HOURS
MAKES 5–6 HELPINGS

1½ oz/40 g dripping or butter
3 lb/1.5 kg middle neck of lamb (in chops)
2 medium onions, chopped
1½ oz/40 g plain flour
1¼ pint/700 ml stock
Salt and freshly ground black pepper
A little sugar
6–7 mushrooms, wiped clean and stalks removed
3 lamb's kidneys, prepared for cooking (see page 17)
3 lb/1.5 kg potatoes

1   Pre-heat the oven to Gas 4/180°C/350°F.

2   Melt the dripping or butter in a frying pan and brown the meat on both sides. Lift out and place in a large casserole.

3   Add the onions to the fat in the frying pan and cook until transparent but not brown. Add the flour and cook for 2–3 minutes until brown. Gradually add the stock and stir carefully until well mixed. Season to taste with salt, pepper and a little sugar.

4   Slice the kidneys thickly and lay on top of the lamb in the casserole. Slice the mushrooms and lay on top. Peel the potatoes and cut into thick slices. Arrange over the mushrooms so that they overlap and completely cover the contents of the casserole.

5   Pour the thickened stock over the potatoes. Cover the casserole and cook in the oven for 2–2¼ hours, then remove the lid and cook for a further 15–20 minutes until the potatoes are golden brown. Serve immediately.

RABBIT STEW

The first time that our five adventurers tasted a really delicious rabbit stew was as a result of an unexpected encounter with a poacher. Out hiking in the country one day, the chums lost their way towards evening and stopped to ask a rather shifty looking chap for directions. At first the fellow seemed reluctant to help, but after a while he became friendlier and even suggested the pals join him for supper. When they assented, he pulled a rabbit from his sack like a magician and prepared the most delicious rabbit stew they had ever tasted.

•

PREPARATION AND COOKING 1½–1¾ HOURS
MAKES 3–4 HELPINGS

2 oz/50 g butter
18 shallot onions, peeled and left whole
4 oz/100 g streaky bacon, diced
1 rabbit, jointed
1½ oz/40 g plain flour
1 pint/600 ml stock
Bouquet garni
2 cloves
Salt and freshly ground black pepper
1 glass of red wine, optional

1   Melt the butter in a large saucepan. Fry the onions and bacon until brown. Lift out with a slotted spoon. Lightly fry the rabbit in the hot fat, sprinkle on the flour and continue cooking until well browned.

2   Replace the onions and bacon, add the stock, bouquet garni, cloves and seasoning. Cover tightly and leave to stew gently for about 1¼–1½ hours until the meat is tender. About 15 minutes before serving add the wine, if using, and leave to finish cooking.

STEAK AND KIDNEY PIE

PREPARATION 45–50 MINUTES, COOKING 1½–2 HOURS
MAKES 5–6 HELPINGS

For the pastry
8 oz/225 g plain flour, sifted
Pinch of salt
6 oz/125 g butter or butter and lard, softened
½ teaspoon lemon juice
Cold water to mix

For the filling
1½ lb/675 g steak and kidney, cut into cubes or narrow strips
¾ oz/20 g plain flour seasoned with salt and freshly ground black pepper
2 onions, peeled and finely chopped
3–4 tablespoons stock or water
1 egg, beaten

1   Make the pastry first. Mix together the flour and salt. Add the butter, cut up into small pieces. Mix lightly with the flour. Make a well in the centre, pour in the lemon juice and gradually add enough water to mix to an elastic dough. Roll out into a long rectangle.

2   Fold in three, seal the edges with the rolling pin, then give the pastry a half turn so that the folded edges are on the right and left. Roll again. Repeat until the pastry has been rolled and folded 4 times, leaving it in the refrigerator for 15 minutes after the second rolling.

3   Pre-heat the oven to Gas 8/230°C/450°F.

4   Toss the meat in the seasoned flour and place with the onions on a pie dish, piling the meat higher in the middle. Sprinkle any remaining flour over the meat. Add enough of the stock or water to quarter-fill the dish.

5   Roll out the pastry to a thickness of ¼–½ in/6–10 mm to roughly the shape of the pie dish, allowing an extra 2 in/5 cm all round. Cut a strip about ¾ in/2 cm wide from around the edge of the pastry to cover the rim of the pie dish.

6   Dampen the rim of the dish and lay the strip around it with the cut side outwards, slightly overlapping the rim. Join the ends firmly. Dampen the pastry rim all over. Lay the pastry lid over the dish and press lid and pastry rim firmly together.

7   Make a small hole in the middle of the pastry, brush all over with beaten egg and place in the oven. Bake for 10–15 minutes, then reduce the heat to Gas 3/170°C/325°F, place the pie on a lower shelf and if necessary cover with greaseproof paper to prevent it burning. Cook for a further 1¼–1½ hours, until the meat is tender.

8   Before serving, heat more stock and pour through the hole in the pastry. Serve the rest separately in a gravy boat.

STEAK AND KIDNEY

PUDDING

PREPARATION AND COOKING 4 HOURS
MAKES 5–6 HELPINGS

**4 oz/100 g shredded suet
8 oz/225 g self-raising flour
1½ lb/700 g steak and kidney, cut into cubes or narrow strips
¾ oz/20 g plain flour seasoned with salt and freshly ground black pepper
3–4 tablespoons stock or water**

1   Grease a 2-pint/1-litre pudding basin.

2   Mix the suet with the flour and add enough cold water to bind together to a stiff dough. Roll out on a floured board to a thickness of about ¼ in/6 mm. Use to line the prepared pudding basin, pressing well in, and leave the spare pastry hanging over the edge.

3   Toss the meat in the seasoned flour, half fill the basin with it, and then add the stock or water. Add the remaining meat. Dampen the edges of the pastry and bring the spare up over the edge of the bowl. Join the edges to enclose the meat completely. Seal really firmly.

4   Cover with greased foil or greaseproof paper and place in a steamer. Place the steamer over a pan of boiling water and cook for about 3½ hours, remembering to top up the boiling water from time to time.

5   Either serve direct from the basin or turn out onto a warmed plate.

TOAD IN THE HOLE

PREPARATION AND COOKING 1 HOUR
MAKES 4 HELPINGS

**4 oz/100 g plain flour
¼ teaspoon salt
1 egg
½ pint/300 ml milk
1 tablespoon cooking fat or beef dripping
1 lb/450 g sausages of your choice**

1   Place the flour and salt in a bowl and make a well in the middle. Break the egg into the well and mix the egg into the flour, gradually adding the milk, and working the flour down from the sides until it is all incorporated. Beat well and leave to stand for ½ hour.

2   Pre-heat the oven to Gas 7/220°C/425°F.

3   Heat the fat in a baking tin or large flat casserole. Place the sausages in the hot fat, then pour the batter in. Bake for 25–30 minutes until set.

STEW AND DOUGHBOYS

PREPARATION AND COOKING 2½–2¾ HOURS
MAKES 5–6 HELPINGS

2 oz/50 g butter or dripping
2 large onions, peeled and roughly chopped
2 lb/900 g good stewing steak, trimmed and cut into 1-in/2.5-cm cubes
2 oz/50 g plain flour
1½ pints/900 ml stock
3 sticks of celery, cut into small pieces
3 carrots, peeled and sliced
Salt and freshly ground black pepper
½ teaspoon paprika
1 teaspoon dried mixed herbs
8–10 oz/225–275 g mushrooms, wiped clean and sliced

For the doughboys
8 oz/225 g self-raising flour
1½–2 tablespoons chopped fresh parsley
Salt and freshly ground black pepper
4 oz/100 g shredded suet
Cold water

1   Pre-heat the oven to Gas 3/170°C/325°F.

2   Heat the fat in a pan and fry the onions with the meat until the meat is well browned. Add the flour and stir until brown. Transfer to an ovenproof casserole, add the stock, celery, carrots, seasoning, paprika and herbs. Stir and cover.

3   Place in the oven and cook for 2 hours, stirring occasionally. Add the mushrooms, stir, and continue cooking for a further 20–30 minutes.

4   Meanwhile make the doughboys (dumplings). Mix the flour, parsley and seasoning in a bowl, then carefully mix in the suet. Add just enough cold water to make a fairly stiff but elastic dough that leaves the bowl clean. Shape into 10–12 dumplings.

5   When the stew is ready, remove the meat and vegetables with a slotted spoon into a warmed serving dish. Cover and keep hot in the oven. Pour the gravy into a saucepan. Bring to the boil and carefully drop in the dumplings. Cover and cook for 20–25 minutes, making quite sure that the pot does not stop boiling.

6   To serve, arrange the dumplings around the meat and pour the gravy over.

Note: If you prefer crisp dumplings, lift the lid of the casserole when the stew is ready, place the dumplings on top of the stew so that they sit in the gravy, and return the casserole to the oven without the lid for 20–25 minutes until the dumplings are golden brown and crispy on top.

SHEPHERD'S PIE

PREPARATION AND COOKING 1¼–2 HOURS
MAKES 5–6 HELPINGS

**Oil or butter for frying
4 onions, peeled and finely chopped
1½ lb/700 g minced beef
1 oz/25 g plain flour
1 teaspoon mixed herbs
Salt and freshly ground black pepper
Stock or water
2½–3 lb/1.25–1.50 kg potatoes, peeled and cut into small pieces**

1   Heat the oil or butter in a large pan. Fry the onions gently until tansparent but not brown. Add the mince and brown well, breaking up with a wooden spoon so that all the meat is browned. Sprinkle over the flour, stir and continue cooking until well browned.

2   Add the herbs, salt and pepper and enough stock or water to barely cover the meat. Leave to simmer for about 1 hour until tender.

3   Meanwhile, place the potatoes in a pan and cover with cold salted water. Bring to the boil and simmer for 10–15 minutes. Strain and mash.

4   Pre-heat the oven to Gas 4/180°C/350°F. Pour the cooked mince into an ovenproof casserole. Carefully spread the mashed potato over the top. Smooth it well and mark a pattern over it with the prongs of a fork. Place in the oven and bake for 30–45 minutes until well browned.

TRIPE AND ONIONS

PREPARATION AND COOKING 2¼ HOURS
MAKES 5–6 HELPINGS

**1½ lb/675 g tripe
½ pint/300 ml milk, plus a little extra
½ pint/300 ml water
1 teaspoon salt
2 large onions, peeled and thinly sliced
A sprig of thyme
1 oz/25 g plain flour
Salt and freshly ground black pepper**

1   Cut the tripe into 2-in/5-cm squares. Put into a saucepan with the milk, water and salt. Add the onions and thyme and bring to the boil. Simmer slowly for 2 hours.

2   Mix the flour to a smooth paste with a little milk, and add to the pan. Stir with a wooden spoon until boiling. Simmer for a further 10 minutes. Season to taste and serve immediately.

ROAST PORK

AND APPLE SAUCE

PREPARATION AND COOKING ABOUT 2 HOURS
MAKES 5–6 HELPINGS

3 lb/1.350 kg loin of pork
1 small onion, peeled and finely chopped
½ teaspoon dried sage
1 teaspoon mustard powder
½ teaspoon salt
Freshly ground black pepper

For the apple sauce
1 lb/450 g cooking apples, peeled and cut into small pieces
2 tablespoons water
½ oz/15 g butter
Rind and juice of ½ lemon
Sugar to taste

1   Pre-heat the oven to Gas 7/220°C/425°F.

2   Score the pork with a very sharp knife to make narrow lines across. Mix together the onion, sage, mustard, salt and pepper and rub into the meat. Wrap the joint in greased greaseproof paper and roast in a covered tin for 10 minutes.

3   Reduce the heat to Gas 4/180°C/350°F and continue cooking for 1 hour 10 minutes. Remove the greaseproof paper and the lid from the baking tin and continue to cook for 30 minutes until the crackling is crisp.

4   Meanwhile make the apple sauce. Stew the apples very gently with the water, butter and lemon rind until soft and pulpy. Beat with a wooden spoon or process or blend until very smooth. Add the lemon juice and reheat. Sweeten to taste. Serve hot with the pork.

ROAST BEEF

AND YORKSHIRE PUD

PREPARATION AND COOKING 1½–1¾ HOURS
MAKES 6 GENEROUS HELPINGS

**2 lb/900 g joint of beef
Salt and freshly ground black pepper
2 oz/50 g beef dripping**

For the Yorkshire pudding
**4 oz/100 g plain flour
1 egg
½ pint/300 ml milk
Salt and freshly ground black pepper**

1   Pre-heat the oven to Gas 8/230°C/450°F.

2   Wipe the joint with a damp cloth. Place in a baking tin with the dripping and put in the hot oven for 10–15 minutes to brown the meat.

3   Reduce the heat to Gas 5/190°C/375°F and cook for 1¼ hours, basting thoroughly every 20 minutes.

4   About 45 minutes before the meat is ready, mix the batter for the Yorkshire pudding. Place the flour and a little seasoning in a bowl. Make a well in the middle, break the eggs into the well and mix gradually into the flour. Gradually add the milk and work the flour down from the sides until it is all incorporated. Beat hard, then leave to stand for 25–30 minutes.

5   About 15 minutes before the meat is ready, spoon a little dripping from the meat pan into a baking tin or individual patty tins. Pour in the batter and place in the oven. Bake until set: 20–30 minutes if in a tin and 10–15 minutes if in patty tins.

6   While the Yorkshire pudding is cooking remove the meat from the pan onto a warmed serving dish and keep warm in the bottom of the oven. Drain the fat from the tin and use the juice from the meat to make gravy by the method described in the recipe for Faggots (page 77).

ROAST CHICKEN
WITH SAGE AND ONION STUFFING

PREPARATION AND COOKING 1¾–2 HOURS
MAKES 5–6 HELPINGS

1 × 3–4 lb/1.5–1.75 kg oven-ready roasting chicken with giblets removed
Salt and freshly ground black pepper
2–3 rashers streaky bacon
½ pint/300 ml chicken stock
Fat or oil for basting

For the stuffing
4 oz/100 g onions, peeled and thickly sliced
½ teaspoon dried powdered sage
2 oz/50 g fresh white breadcrumbs
1 oz/25 g butter, softened
Salt and freshly ground black pepper
1 egg

1　Pre-heat the oven to Gas 5–6/190–200°C/375–400°F.

2　Make the stuffing first. Place the onions in a pan with just enough cold water to barely cover. Bring to the boil and simmer for 10 minutes. Drain and chop finely or run through a food processor for a few seconds.

3　Mix the onions with the sage, breadcrumbs, butter, seasoning and egg, and mix well together. Press the stuffing into the chicken.

4　Lay the chicken in a baking tin. Season lightly and lay the rashers of bacon over the top. Roast for 1½–1¾ hours until tender, basting frequently. To test for tenderness, prick the thigh with a skewer. If there is any trace of blood the meat is not cooked.

5　About 10–15 minutes before the chicken is cooked, remove the bacon to allow the breast to brown. When it is ready remove from the oven and lift carefully onto a warmed serving dish. Remove any string and keep the bird hot.

6　Skim off any excess fat from the baking tin, but keep the juices. Put the tin on top of the stove, pour in the stock so that it mixes with the juices and boil for 2–3 minutes. Season to taste and serve separately in a gravy boat.

FAGGOTS

PREPARATION AND COOKING 1–1¼ HOURS
MAKES 5–6 HELPINGS

1 lb/450 g liver
2 medium onions
4 oz/100 g fatty pork
Pinch each of thyme and basil
½ teaspoon dried sage
Salt and freshly ground black pepper
Pinch of grated nutmeg
1 egg
Breadcrumbs, fresh, white or brown

For the gravy
1 oz/25 g butter
1 oz/25 g plain flour
Stock from the stewed meats

1   Slice the liver, onions and pork thinly. Place in a saucepan with the herbs, seasoning and nutmeg. Add enough water to just cover. Bring to the boil and simmer for ½-hour. Strain off the liquid and reserve.

2   Put the contents of the pan in a food processor (or through a mincer) until finely chopped. Add the egg and enough breadcrumbs to make a firm mixture. Blend well together.

3   Pre-heat the oven to Gas 6/200°C/400°F. Form the mixture into balls and wrap each in a piece of foil. Place in a baking tray and bake for 25–30 minutes until well browned.

4   Meanwhile make the gravy. Melt the butter, add the flour and stir over a moderate heat for 2–3 minutes. Remove from the heat and gradually add the stock. Return to the stove and stir until the gravy thickens.

5   Remove the foil from the faggots. Pour the gravy over and serve immediately.

BOILED BEEF

AND CARROTS

PREPARATION AND COOKING 1½–1¾ HOURS
MAKES 5–6 HELPINGS

**2½–3 lb/1.25–1.50 kg unsalted silverside, brisket or round of beef, tied with
string into a neat shape
1 teaspoon salt
3 cloves
10 black peppercorns
A bunch of fresh mixed herbs or 2 teaspoons dried mixed herbs
1 lb/450 g carrots, peeled and sliced
1 lb/450 g turnips, peeled and sliced
1 lb/450 g onions, peeled and sliced**

1   Place the meat in a large pan, cover with boiling water and add the salt. Bring to the boil and boil for 5 minutes to seal the outside of the meat. Reduce the heat to simmer, add the cloves, peppercorns and herbs and simmer for approximately 1 hour. Skim off any froth as necessary.

2   Add the sliced vegetables and simmer for a further 20 minutes until the vegetables are tender.

3   Lift out the meat and place on a hot serving dish. Remove the string. Lift the vegetables out of the pan with a slotted spoon and arrange neatly around the meat. Serve the gravy separately, or save as stock for soup.

Note: Other vegetables can be added if preferred – celery, parsnips, swedes etc. all go very well with the beef.

LIVER AND ONIONS

PREPARATION AND COOKING 1 HOUR
MAKES 5–6 HELPINGS

**1½–1¾ lb/675–800 g lamb's or calves' liver
2–3 large onions, peeled and sliced
Salt and freshly ground black pepper
2 oz/50 g plain flour, seasoned with salt and pepper
2 oz/50 g butter**

1   Pre-heat the oven to Gas 3/170°C/325°F.

2   Place the onions in a pan, cover with cold water, add ½ teaspoon salt and bring to the boil. Boil for 4–5 minutes, then drain.

3   Cut the liver into slices and coat with the seasoned flour. Melt the butter in a frying pan and fry the slices for a few minutes on both sides until well browned. Remove from the pan with a slotted spoon and place in an oven-proof casserole.

4   Lay the onions on top. Add enough stock or water to barely cover. Add a little salt and pepper. Cover the casserole and cook in the oven for 45–50 minutes. Serve immdediately with mashed or baked potatoes.

OXTAIL STEW

PREPARATION AND COOKING 3–3½ HOURS
MAKES 5–6 HELPINGS

**2 oz/50 g fat
2 oxtails, cut into joints and with all fat removed
2 onions, sliced
1½ oz/40 g flour
1½ pints/900 ml stock
Salt and freshly ground black pepper
1 bouquet garni
2–3 cloves
Pinch of ground mace
Juice of ½ lemon**

1   Melt the fat in a large pan and fry the oxtail pieces until brown. Remove from the pan with a slotted spoon.

2   Fry the onions in the fat left in the pan until lightly browned. Add the flour, mix well and fry slowly until a good brown colour. Add the stock, seasoning, bouquet garni, cloves and mace, and bring to the boil.

3   Return the oxtail pieces to the pan and simmer gently for 2½–3 hours. Remove the meat from the pan and lay on a hot serving dish. Add the lemon juice to the sauce, and adjust seasoning if necessary, then remove the bouquet garni. Pour over the meat.

6

What's For
Pud?

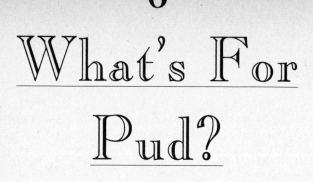

OUR five heroes were just devouring the last scrummy morsels of the most enormous stew with doughboys that Bennett had prepared, when Patterson smacked his lips and said, 'Capital nosh, Bennett! What's for pud?'

Bennett looked startled. 'My hat!' he said, 'I forgot all about pud! Crumbs – what shall we do?' 'Not to worry, chaps,' said Caruthers, 'there's bound to be flour and eggs in the pantry. We'll knock up some pancakes. Any objections?'

They all agreed it was a spiffing idea so they hunted around in the pantry for the necessary supplies and Bennett mixed a first-rate batter.

They chaps waited in eager anticipation as Bennett expertly prepared a pile of mouthwatering pancakes, tossing each one into the air with aplomb. Needless to say, there were hoots of laughter when he misjudged a throw and one of the pancakes landed messily on the floor! Poor old Bennett really felt quite a chump!

CRUNDLEY APPROACHED THE
PROFITEROLES WITH SOME DEGREE
OF TREPIDATION

Despite having polished off the stew and dumplings, they consumed 30 pancakes between them, then leaned back in their chairs, disinclined to move. 'It's a jolly good job we're off on a long hike tomorrow,' ventured Morrell. 'We need a thundering good day's exercise after that little feast.' 'Dashed tasty grub, though!' murmured Caruthers.

ACCIDENT IN THE ALPS

(RICE PUDDING AND JAM)

The pals adore rice pudding, especially when it's coated in lashings of bright red jam. Bennett caused much hilarity one lunchtime when he commented that his plateful of rice pudding and jam resembled some awful skiing accident! Since then the chaps have always referred to this tasty dish as 'Accident in the Alps'!

•

PREPARATION AND COOKING 2½–3 HOURS
MAKES 5–6 HELPINGS

4 oz/100 g pudding rice
2 pints/1 litre milk
2–3 oz/50–75 g caster sugar
½ oz butter
Red jam

1   Grease a pie dish. Wash the rice in cold water and place in the dish with the milk. Leave to stand for ½ hour.

2   Pre-heat the oven to Gas 2/150°C/310°F.

3   Add the sugar to the rice, flake the butter and sprinkle over. Bake for 2–2½ hours until the pudding is thick and creamy and brown on top.

4   Serve with a generous dollop of red jam in the middle of each plateful.

Variations
Tapioca or sago pudding can be made in exactly the same way, with the addition of a little ground nutmeg or cinnamon.

SEMOLINA
OR GROUND RICE PUDDING

PREPARATION AND COOKING 40 MINUTES
MAKES 5–6 HELPINGS

**2 pints/1 litre milk
3 oz/75 g semolina or ground rice
2–3 oz/50–75 g sugar
A little ground nutmeg**

1   Heat the milk to nearly boiling. Sprinkle the semolina or ground rice over and stir quickly to prevent lumps from forming. Place over the heat and simmer, stirring continuously, for about 15 minutes, until the grain is transparent. Add the sugar and nutmeg.

2   Meanwhile heat the oven to Gas 4/180°C/350°F and butter a pie dish. Pour the mixture into the dish and bake for 20–30 minutes until the top has browned.

APPLE CHARLOTTE

PREPARATION AND COOKING 1–1¼ HOURS
MAKES 5–6 HELPINGS

**2 lb/900 g cooking apples, peeled, cored and sliced
4 oz/100 g brown sugar
Grated rind and juice of 1 lemon
8 slices of white or brown buttered bread
Caster sugar for dredging**

1   Pre-heat the oven to Gas 4/180°C/350°F

2   Butter a 2-pint/1-litre ovenproof dish and place a layer of apples in the bottom. Sprinkle with a little of the sugar, lemon rind and juice, then cover with slices of bread. Repeat the layers until the dish is full, finishing with a layer of bread.

3   Cover with greased greaseproof paper and bake for 45 minutes to 1 hour.

4   Remove from the oven, dredge with caster sugar and serve. Alternatively turn the pudding out onto a serving dish and then dredge with sugar.

APPLE CRUMBLE

PREPARATION AND COOKING 40–50 MINUTES
MAKES 5–6 HELPINGS

2 lb/900 g cooking apples, peeled, cored and sliced
7 oz/100 g demerara sugar
A little grated lemon rind
A little water
3 oz/75 g butter or margarine, softened
6 oz/175 g plain flour
3 oz/75 g sugar
Pinch of mixed spice or nutmeg
Caster sugar for dredging

1   Pre-heat the oven to Gas 4/180°C/350°F.

2   Place the apples in a saucepan with a little water, 4 oz/100 g of the sugar and the lemon rind. Cook gently with the lid on until soft. Pour into a 2-pint/1 litre pie dish or casserole.

3   Rub the fat into the flour until the mixture resembles fine breadcrumbs. Add the remaining sugar and the spice and mix well. Sprinkle over the top of the apples.

4   Bake for 30–40 minutes until the crumble is golden brown. Remove from the oven, sprinkle a little caster sugar over the top and serve hot or cold with custard or cream.

Variations
Other fruits are equally good for crumble. For example, rhubarb, apricots, plums, damsons etc. Stew in the same way before putting into the pie dish. Rhubarb and date crumble, with a little ginger for those who like it, is particularly scrumptious.

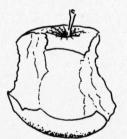

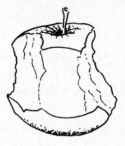

APPLE PIE

PREPARATION AND COOKING 45 MINUTES–1 HOUR
MAKES 5–6 HELPINGS

For the pastry
6 oz/175 g plain flour, sifted
3 oz/75 g butter or margarine, softened
1–2 tablespoons cold water

For the filling
1½ lb/750 g cooking apples, peeled, cored and sliced
3 oz/75 g soft brown or demerara sugar
½ teaspoon ground cinnamon or mixed spice
4 cloves
Milk and caster sugar to glaze

1   Pre-heat the oven to Gas 5/190°C/375°F. Place the flour in a bowl. Rub in the fat until the mixture resembles breadcrumbs. Add enough water to mix to a firm dough. Turn out onto a floured board and knead lightly for a minute or two.

2   Place the prepared apples in a 1½ pint/900 ml pie dish and sprinkle the sugar over.

3   Roll out the pastry to a thickness of approximately ¼ in/6 mm and about 2 in/5 cm larger in diameter than the dish. Cut off a strip about 1 in/2.5 cm all around and use to cover the rim of the dish. Dampen with a little water.

4   Place the pastry circle over the top of the apples and seal the edges. Trim off any surplus pastry and press all around the rim with a knife blade to make a fluted pattern. Make a small hole in the middle of the pastry. Brush the top with a little milk and sprinkle over a little sugar.

5   Bake for 30–40 minutes until lightly golden. Remove, sprinkle with a little more caster sugar and serve hot or cold.

APPLE DUMPLINGS

PREPARATION AND COOKING 50–60 MINUTES
MAKES 6 HELPINGS

8 oz/225 g plain flour, sifted
Pinch of salt
2 oz/50 g butter, softened
2 oz/50 g lard, softened
1 teaspoon baking powder
A little cold water
6 cooking apples
2 oz/50 g demerara or soft brown sugar and a little caster sugar for
sprinkling
1 teaspoon ground cinnamon
A little milk
3 oz/75 g of any of the following, alone or mixed:
currants, raisins, sultanas, chopped dates and walnuts

1   Make the pastry first. Mix the flour and salt together. Rub in the fat, add the baking powder and, using a knife, mix to a stiff dough with a little cold water.

2   Pre-heat the oven to Gas 6/200°C/400°F. Wash and core the apples. Cut around the skin one third of the way down with the tip of a sharp knife. On a floured surface, roll the pastry out to a thickness of ¼ in/ 6 mm and cut into 6 squares. Place an apple in the middle of each.

3   Make the filling by mixing together about 1½ oz/40 g of the brown sugar, the cinnamon, the milk and the dried fruit. Fill the centres of the apples with it, then sprinkle the tops with the remaining sugar.

4   Brush the edges of the pastry with a little water, bring the pastry up around the apples and seal carefully. Place in a baking tin and brush all over with milk. Sprinkle with a little caster sugar. Bake for 30–40 minutes. Serve hot with custard.

APPLE FRITTERS

PREPARATION 40 MINUTES, COOKING 4–5 MINUTES FOR EACH FRITTER
MAKES 9–10 FRITTERS

4 oz/100 g plain flour, sifted
Pinch of salt
Pinch of sugar
1 egg
¼ pint/150 ml milk
2 apples, peeled, cored and cut in rings or slices
Oil for frying
Caster sugar for dredging
Lemon wedges

1   Mix together the flour, salt and sugar. Make a well in the middle and break the egg into it. Add a little milk and gradually mix the flour into the egg and milk, working the flour down from the sides of the bowl.

2   Gradually add the rest of the milk and beat well. Leave to stand for 30 minutes.

3   Heat about 1 in/2.5 cm of oil in a frying pan until just smoking. Coat each apple ring with batter and drop very carefully into the oil. Cook until golden brown, turning so that both sides are evenly cooked. Lift out with a slotted spoon and drain on kitchen paper. Keep warm. Repeat until all the apple rings are cooked.

4   To serve, dredge with caster sugar and squeeze lemon juice over.

BAKED APPLES

PREPARATION 5–10 MINUTES, COOKING 45 MINUTES TO 1 HOUR
MAKES 6 HELPINGS

6 cooking apples, washed and cored
3 oz/75 g of any of the following, alone or mixed: currants, sultanas, raisins,
chopped dates and walnuts mixed with 2 oz/50 g demerara or soft brown
sugar and 1 teaspoon ground cinnamon
2 oz/50 g demerara or soft brown sugar
A little cold water

1   Pre-heat the oven to Gas 4/180°C/350°F.

2   Cut around the skin of the apples one-third of the way down with the tip of a sharp knife. Place them in an ovenproof casserole or dish and fill the centres with the mixed filling. Sprinkle the 2 oz/50 g of sugar over the top. Add a little water.

3   Bake for 45 minutes to 1 hour until the apples are soft. Serve hot or cold with custard.

BANANA CUSTARD

PREPARATION 15 MINUTES, INCLUDING THE CUSTARD
MAKES 5 HELPINGS

5 bananas
1 pint/600 ml custard (see page 92)
5 tablespoons strawberry or other jam

1   Remove the skin from the bananas and split each lengthways.
Spread each half with strawberry jam.

2   Lay the banana halves together again. Arrange neatly in a serving
dish or bowl, and pour the custard over. For extra indulgence serve with
whipped cream.

BANANA SPLIT

PREPARATION 10–15 MINUTES INCLUDING THE SAUCE
MAKES 6 HELPINGS

6 bananas
1 pint/600 ml vanilla ice-cream
¼ pint/150 ml double cream
1 teaspoon caster sugar
2 oz/50 g maraschino cherries
1 oz/25 g chopped walnuts

For the melba sauce
1 lb/450 g raspberries
2 tablespoons icing sugar

1   Peel the bananas and split in half lengthways. Place in small oval
dishes. Place 2 scoops or slices of ice-cream between the two halves.

2   Make the melba sauce next. Press the raspberries through a sieve
and blend the pulp with the icing sugar.

3   Coat the ice-cream with the melba sauce. Sprinkle with the cherries
and nuts.

BAKEWELL TART

PREPARATION AND COOKING 45 MINUTES
MAKES 5–6 HELPINGS

For the pastry
4 oz/100 g plain flour
Pinch of salt
½ teaspoon baking powder
1 oz/25 g butter, softened
1 oz/25 g lard, softened
Cold water

For the filling
3–4 tablespoons raspberry jam
2 oz/50 g butter, softened
2 oz/50 g caster sugar
1 egg
Few drops of almond essence
1½ oz/40 g ground almonds
½ oz/15 g self-raising flour

1   Sift the flour, salt and baking powder together. Rub in the fat and, using a knife, mix to a stiff dough with cold water. Roll out on a floured surface to a thickness of ¼ in/6 mm.

2   Pre-heat the oven to Gas 5/190°C/375°F and grease a 7-in/18-cm pie plate. Use the pastry to line the plate and trim off any surplus. Spread the jam over the pastry.

3   Beat together the butter and sugar until light and fluffy. Add the egg and beat well. Add the almond essence, ground almonds and flour. Mix together thoroughly. Spread over the jam.

4   Bake for about 30 minutes. Serve hot or cold, alone or with custard or cream.

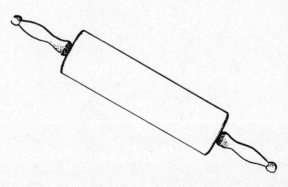

BATTER PUDDING

This is delicious with plenty of jam, syrup or maple syrup poured over!

•

PREPARATION 35–40 MINUTES, COOKING 30–40 MINUTES
MAKES 5–6 HELPINGS

8 oz/225 g plain flour, sifted
½ teaspoon caster sugar
Pinch of salt
2 eggs
1 pint/600 ml milk
1 tablespoon cooking fat or oil

1   Mix together the flour, sugar and salt. Make a well in the centre and break the eggs in. Add a little of the milk and gradually mix the flour into the eggs, working it down from the sides of the bowl. Add more milk as required to make a stiff batter. Beat hard, then leave to stand for 30 minutes.

2   Meanwhile, pre-heat the oven to Gas 7/220°C/425°F. Pour a little fat or oil into a Yorkshire pudding tin and heat in the oven until just beginning to smoke. Quickly pour in the batter and leave to cook at the top of the oven for 20–25 minutes, until browned.

3   Reduce the heat to Gas 5/190°C/375°F and cook for a further 10–15 minutes until cooked through.

APPLE BATTER PUD

PREPARATION 35–40 MINUTES, COOKING 35–40 MINUTES
MAKES 5–6 HELPINGS

8 oz/225 g plain flour
½ teaspoon caster sugar
Pinch of salt
2 eggs
1 pint/600 ml milk
1 lb/400 g apples, peeled, cored and sliced
2 oz/50 g soft brown sugar
¼ teaspoon ground cinnamon
½ oz/15 g butter
Caster sugar for dredging

1   Prepare the batter exactly as for Batter pudding (see page 90).

2   Pre-heat the oven to gas 7/220°C/425°F and grease a casserole.

3   Place the prepared apples in the casserole with the sugar and spice. Pour the batter over and flake the butter over the top.

4   Bake for 20–25 minutes until brown. Reduce the heat to Gas 5/190°C/375°F and cook for a further 10–15 minutes. Dredge with caster sugar and serve immediately.

BREAD AND BUTTER

PUDDING

PREPARATION 35–40 MINUTES, COOKING 1 HOUR
MAKES 5–6 HELPINGS

8 slices of buttered bread
2 oz/50 g sultanas, currants or raisins (or a mixture)
1 oz/25 g mixed peel
1½ oz/35 g sugar
3 eggs
1½ pint/900 ml milk

1   Grease a 2-pint/1-litre pie dish.

2   Cut the bread into squares and use some of the squares to cover the bottom of the dish. Sprinkle over some of the fruit and peel and a little sugar. Repeat the layers until all the ingredients are used up.

3   Beat eggs and milk and pour over the bread. Leave to soak for 30 minutes.

4   Meanwhile heat the oven to Gas 4/180°C/350°F. Bake the pudding for about 1 hour until the custard is set.

CUSTARD

PREPARATION 10 MINUTES
MAKES 1 PINT/60 ML

2 rounded tablespoons custard powder
2 rounded tablespoons granulated sugar
1 pint/600 ml milk

1   Thoroughly mix the custard powder and sugar with 2 tablespoons of the milk.

2   Put the rest of the milk in a pan and bring to the boil. When boiling pour onto the custard powder and mix really well.

3   Return the mixture to the pan and boil for 1 minute, stirring all the time. Pour into a jug or serving bowl.

Extra hints:
- To stop the custard from forming a skin, sprinkle a little caster sugar over the top; this can then be stirred in just before using.
- To give the custard a specially creamy taste, use slightly less milk, and when cooked, stir in 2 tablespoons of double cream. Blend in thoroughly.
- Add a few drops of almond essence just before pouring the custard into the jug or serving bowl.
- For thick custard, use a little extra custard powder; for thin custard use a little less.

CUSTARD SAUCE

PREPARATION 10–15 MINUTES
MAKES ½ PINT/300 ML

2 egg yolks
2 teaspoons sugar
½ pint/300 ml milk
½ teaspoon ground nutmeg, cinnamon or lemon peel

1   Beat the egg yolks lightly and beat in the sugar. Warm the milk to blood heat, then stir into the egg mixture.

2   Return to the pan and heat very gently, stirring all the time, until the custard thickens. It must not boil or the egg will curdle. As soon as it thickens pour through a strainer or sieve into a sauce boat or serving bowl. Add extra sugar if necessary.

CUSTARD PIE

PREPARATION AND COOKING ABOUT 1¼ HOURS
MAKES 7–8 HELPINGS

For the pastry
6 oz/175 g plain flour
3 oz/75 g butter or margarine
1–2 tablespoons cold water

For the custard
2 eggs
½ oz/15 g caster sugar
½ pint/300 ml milk
½ teaspoon nutmeg

1   Pre-heat the oven to gas 6/200°C/400°F and grease an 8-in/20-cm flan dish. Sift the flour into a bowl. Rub in the fat until the mixture resembles breadcrumbs. Add enough water to mix to a firm dough. Turn onto a floured board and knead lightly. Roll out to a thickness of about ¼ in/6 mm and line the flan ring with the pastry. Trim off any surplus.

2   Place a circle of greaseproof paper inside the pie case with a layer of dried beans on top. Bake the pie case 'blind' for 15–20 minutes, remove the beans and the paper and cook for a further 5 minutes. Lower the oven heat to Gas 3/170°C/325°F.

3   To make the custard, beat the eggs with the sugar. Warm the milk slightly and add gradually to the egg mixture, stirring well. Pour the custard into the pie case. Sprinkle the nutmeg over the top.

4   Bake the pie for 45–50 minutes, until the custard is set. Remove from the oven and leave to cool. Serve slightly warm or cold.

SWEET WHITE SAUCE

PREPARATION 10 MINUTES
MAKES 1 PINT/600 ML

2 tablespoons cornflour
2 tablespoons granulated sugar
1 pint/600 ml milk

1   Mix the cornflour and sugar with 2 tablespoons of the milk and blend thoroughly.

2   Bring the rest of the milk to the boil. When boiling pour over the cornflour and stir well. Return the sauce to the pan and boil for 1 minute, stirring all the time. Pour into a jug or serving bowl.

Note: The sauce can be coloured by adding a few drops of food colouring.

CHOCOLATE SAUCE

This is excellent for pouring over chocolate sponge pudding or over ice-cream.

●

PREPARATION 10 MINUTES
MAKES 1 PINT/600 ML

1 rounded tablespoon cornflour
2 rounded tablespoons cocoa powder
3 rounded tablespoons sugar
1 pint/600 ml water
6 drops vanilla essence
½ oz/15 g butter

1   Blend together the cornflour, cocoa and sugar with 2 tablespoons of the water. Bring the rest of the water to the boil. When boiling pour onto the cocoa mixture. Stir well.

2   Return to the pan and boil for 2 minutes, stirring all the time. Add the vanilla and butter and stir. Serve hot or cold.

GANGES MUD

(CHOCOLATE BLANCMANGE)

The students of Mannington have always referred to Chocolate Blancmange as 'Ganges Mud'. This version, created by the pals as an improvement on Cook's average blancmange, is a decidedly superior version.

●

PREPARATION AND COOKING 5 MINUTES
MAKES 4–5 HELPINGS

8 oz/225 g plain chocolate, broken into small pieces
1 pint/600 ml milk
2 tablespoons sugar
2 tablespoons cornflour

1   Melt the chocolate with 3 tablespoons of the milk. Don't let it become more than lukewarm.

2   Mix the sugar and cornflour with a little of the remaining milk and stir well.

3   Bring the rest of the milk to the boil. Pour onto the cornflour, mix thoroughly, return to the pan and bring back to the boil, stirring continuously until thickened.

4   Blend the chocolate into the mixture. Stir well, pour into a serving dish and leave to cool.

JAM ROLY-POLY

PREPARATION 15 MINUTES, COOKING 2–2½ HOURS
MAKES 5–6 HELPINGS

**12 oz/350 g plain flour
2 teaspoons baking powder
Pinch of salt
6 oz/175 g shredded suet**

For the jam sauce
**4 heaped tablespoons jam of your choice
½ pint/300 ml water
1½ teaspoons arrowroot**

1   Mix together the flour, baking powder, salt and suet, and add enough cold water to mix to a soft but firm dough.

2   On a floured board roll out the pastry to a thickness of ¼ in/6 mm. Spread with plenty of jam, almost to the edges. Dampen the edges with a little water and roll up lightly, sealing the edges carefully.

3   Wrap the pudding in a well-floured cloth. Tie up the ends, put into fast-boiling water, and simmer for 2–2½ hours. Remove from the water, untie the cloth and place on a warmed serving dish.

4   Make the jam sauce. Place all the ingredients together in a pan and heat gently, stirring all the time, until the sauce thickens.

5   Serve with custard (see page 92).

STEWED RHUBARB

AND CUSTARD

PREPARATION 10–15 MINUTES, COOKING 45 MINUTES
MAKES 4 HELPINGS

**1 lb/450 g rhubarb
Juice of 1 lemon
3 tablespoons brown sugar**

1   Pre-heat the oven to Gas 4/180°C/350°F.

2   Cut the rhubarb into 1–2-in/2.5–5 cm length pieces. Place in a casserole with the sugar and lemon juice. Bake for about 45 minutes or until the fruit is tender.

3   Make the custard as described on page 92.

STEWED APPLES

OR PEARS

PREPARATION 10–15 MINUTES, COOKING 45 MINUTES TO 1 HOUR
MAKES 4 HELPINGS

**1 lb/450 g apples or pears
3–4 tablespoons sugar
Cold water
Cloves or cinnamon, optional**

1   Pre-heat the oven to Gas 4/180°C/350°F.

2   Peel and core the fruit and cut into quarters or slices. Place in a pan or casserole with the sugar and water. Add two or three cloves, if liked, to the apples, or a little cinnamon (or a cinnamon stick) to the pears. Bake for 45 minutes to 1 hour until the fruit is tender.

PANCAKES

PREPARATION 35–40 MINUTES, COOKING 4–5 MINUTES FOR EACH PANCAKE
MAKES 9–10

**8 oz/225 g plain flour, sifted
¼ teaspoon caster sugar, plus extra for dredging
2 eggs
1 pint/600 ml milk
Lard or oil for frying
1 lemon**

1   Mix together the flour, salt and sugar. Make a well in the centre and break the eggs in. Add a little milk and gradually mix the flour into the eggs, working the flour down from the sides of the bowl. Gradually add the rest of the milk and beat well. Leave to stand for 30 minutes.

2   Brush the frying pan with a little fat or oil and heat until just beginning to smoke. Quickly pour enough batter into the pan to coat the bottom very thinly, tilting the pan to make sure the batter is spread evenly.

3   When the pancake is set, and brown underneath, loosen the edges with a palette knife. Toss the pancake and cook the other side until golden. Slide onto a serving plate, sprinkle with lemon juice and dredge with caster sugar. Roll up and eat immediately!

Other fillings for pancakes
• Spread with jam before rolling
• Make a purée with stewed apples and mix with raisins and a little cinnamon. Spread on the pancakes and roll up

SPOTTED DICK

PREPARATION 10 MINUTES, COOKING 2–2½ HOURS
MAKES 5–6 HELPINGS

**12 oz/350 g plain flour, sifted
2 teaspoons baking powder
6 oz/175 g shredded suet
Pinch of salt
6 oz/175 g caster sugar
6 oz/175 g currants (or a mixture of currants, raisins and sultanas)**

1   Mix together all the ingredients and add enough water to mix to a soft but firm dough.

2   Roll out to a rectangle about ¼ in/6 mm thick. Dampen the edges, then roll up lightly. Seal the edges.

3   Wrap the pudding in a well-floured cloth. Tie up the ends and put into fast-boiling water to cook for 2–2½ hours. Serve with custard (see page 92).

STODGY GOLDEN SPONGE

PREPARATION 10–15 MINUTES, COOKING 1½–2 HOURS
MAKES 6–7 HELPINGS

**4 tablespoons golden syrup, plus extra to serve if liked
6 oz/175 g plain flour
6 oz/175 g breadcrumbs
4 oz/100 g shredded suet
2 oz/50 g caster sugar
1 teaspoon ground ginger
1 teaspoon bicarbonate of soda
Pinch of salt
1 egg
1 tablespoon treacle
A little milk**

1   Grease a 2½-pint/1.4-litre basin and place 2 tablespoons golden syrup in the bottom.

2   Mix together the dry ingredients.

3   Beat the egg with a further 2 tablespoons golden syrup, the treacle and a little milk. Stir into the other ingredients, adding a little more milk to form to a soft dropping consistency.

4   Pour into the basin and cover with a piece of greaseproof paper or foil. Place in a steamer over a pan of boiling water and cook for 1½–2 hours, remembering to top up the boiling water from time to time.

5   Turn out onto a warmed serving dish and serve with extra syrup.

LEMON MERINGUE PIE

PREPARATION AND COOKING 1–1¼ HOURS
MAKES 5–6 HELPINGS

For the pastry
6 oz/175 g plain flour
3 oz/75 g butter or margarine
1–2 tablespoons cold water

For the filling
4 tablespoons cornflour
½ pint/300 ml water
1 oz/25 g butter
Grated rind and juice of 2 lemons
2 eggs, separated
6 oz/175 g caster sugar

1   Pre-heat the oven to Gas 6/200°C/400°F.

2   Make the pastry first. Sift the flour into a bowl. Rub in the fat and mix to a firm dough with cold water.

3   Turn onto a floured surface, roll out to a circle approximately 7 in/ 18 cm, and use to line a 7-in/18-cm flat pie dish or flan ring. Trim the edge and place a circle of greaseproof paper on top. Place a layer of dried beans on the paper and bake the pastry case 'blind' for 15–20 minutes, then remove the paper and beans and return to the oven for a further 5 minutes. Remove from the oven and leave to cool. Reduce the oven temperature to Gas 3/170°C/325°F.

4   In a small pan blend the cornflour with a little of the cold water. Add the remaining water and mix well. Add the butter and bring to the boil, stirring constantly. Cook for 3 minutes, stirring. Remove from the heat and add the lemon juice and rind, egg yolks and 2 oz/50 g of the sugar. Pour into the flan case.

5   Whisk the egg whites until very stiff. Add 2 oz/50 g of the sugar and whisk again. Fold in the remaining sugar.

6   Spread the meringue over the filling and bake for 20–25 minutes. Serve hot or cold with cream.

TRIFLE

This is not absolutely a traditional English trifle but the five pals have always preferred this ever since Morrell's Aunt Louisa made it for a garden party one summer!

•

PREPARATION 2–3 HOURS, INCLUDING TIME TO SET
MAKES 7–8 HELPINGS

1 packet trifle sponges
3–4 tablespoons medium sweet sherry
2–3 tablespoons raspberry jam
2 × 13.6 oz/385 g tins raspberries
1½ tablets raspberry jelly
1 × 13.6 oz/385 g tin sliced peaches
1 pint/600 ml custard (see page 92)
1 pint/600 ml double cream, whipped
Glacé cherries or jelly diamonds to decorate

1   Put the trifle sponges in a large serving bowl and pour the sherry over them. Leave to soak for 10–15 minutes. Stir in the jam.

2   Drain the juice from the raspberries into a small pan and add the raspberry jelly. Warm gently until the jelly has dissolved. Leave to cool for 10–15 minutes, then pour over the sponges and stir well.

3   Drain the juice from the peaches and add the peach slices and raspberries to the mixture. Turn carefully to distribute the fruit evenly. Place in the refrigerator to set.

4   Make the custard and leave to cool slightly to prevent it melting the jelly. Pour over the top of the trifle and leave to cool.

5   Put the whipped cream into a piping bag with a wide star nozzle, and pipe cream all over the top of the trifle. Alternatively, spread it over with a knife and make a pattern in it with the prongs of a fork. Decorate with glacé cherries or jelly diamonds.

STEAMED JAM SPONGE

PREPARATION 10 MINUTES, COOKING 1½–2 HOURS
MAKES 5–6 HELPINGS

**3 tablespoons red jam
6 oz/175 g plain flour
Pinch of salt
1¼ teaspoon baking powder
2 oz/50 g butter or margarine, softened
2 oz/50 g caster sugar
A few drops of vanilla essence
1 egg, beaten
A little milk**

1   Grease a 2-pint/1-litre pudding basin and place the jam in the bottom.

2   Sift together the flour, salt and baking powder, rub in the fat and add the sugar. Mix to a dropping consistency with the vanilla essence, egg and milk.

3   Pour into the greased basin and cover the top of the basin with a piece of greaseproof paper or foil. Place in a steamer over a pan of boiling water and cook for 1½–2 hours, remembering to top up the boiling water from time to time.

4   When ready, turn out onto a warmed serving dish and serve with extra jam.

STEAMED
CHOCOLATE SPONGE

Make as for jam sponge but omit the jam, and use 4 oz/100 g flour with 2 oz/50 g cocoa. Serve with chocolate sauce (see page 94), sweet white sauce (see page 93) – or custard (see page 92).

LIGHT GOLDEN SPONGE

Make exactly as for jam sponge but spoon 2–3 tablespoons golden syrup into the basin, and serve with more, warmed syrup!

QUEEN OF PUDDINGS

PREPARATION AND COOKING 1¼–2 HOURS
MAKES 5–6 HELPINGS

1 pint/600 ml milk
½ pint/300 ml fresh white breadcrumbs
2 oz/50 g butter or margarine
Grated rind of 2 lemons
2 oz/50 g granulated sugar
2 eggs, separated
3–4 tablespoons jam
3–4 oz/75–100 g caster sugar

1   Heat the milk and add the breadcrumbs, fat, lemon rind and sugar. Leave to soak for 30 minutes.

2   Pre-heat the oven to gas 4/180°C/350°F and grease a pie dish.

3   Stir the egg yolks into the milk mixture. Pour the mixture into the dish and bake for about 45 minutes.

4   Remove the dish from the oven and spread the jam over the pudding. Reduce the oven to Gas ½/130°C/265°F.

5   Whip the egg whites stiffly, add 1 oz/25 g of the sugar and whip again until stiff. Fold in the rest of the sugar and spread over the pudding. Leave in the very cool oven until the meringue is set and golden brown.

FIGGY PUDDING

PREPARATION 10–15 MINUTES, COOKING 2½ HOURS
MAKES 6 HELPINGS

8 oz/225 g dried figs, chopped small
Juice and grated rind of 1 lemon
4 oz/100 g plain flour
1 teaspoon baking powder
2 teaspoons mixed spice
4 oz/100 g fresh white breadcrumbs
4 oz/100 g shredded suet
3 oz/75 g soft brown sugar
2 eggs, beaten
2 tablespoons milk
Golden syrup, to serve

1   Grease a 2-pint/1-litre pudding basin.

2   Mix the figs with the lemon rind and 3 tablespoons of the juice.

3   Sift together the flour, baking powder, spice, breadcrumbs, suet and sugar and mix well.

4   Beat in the fig mixture and the egg, and add enough milk to give a soft dropping consistency. Spoon into the prepared basin and cover with greaseproof paper or foil. Steam for 2½ hours, until well risen and firm.

5   Turn out onto a warm serving plate. Spoon warmed syrup all over and serve with custard (see page 92) or sweet white sauce (see page 93).

UPSIDE-DOWN PUDDING

PREPARATION 10–15 MINUTES, COOKING 40–45 MINUTES
MAKES 4–5 HELPINGS

5 oz/125 g margarine or butter
5 oz/125 g soft brown sugar
4 fresh or tinned pears or peaches, peeled, halved and de-stoned, or
pineapple rings.
4 oz/100 g margarine or butter
2 eggs
4 oz/100 g self-raising flour
1 teaspoon cinnamon or other spice

1   Pre-heat the oven to Gas 5/190°C/375°F and grease and line a 7-in/18-cm round cake tin.

2   Beat together the 1 oz/25 g of the fat and 1 oz/25 g of the sugar and spread onto the bottom of the tin. Lay the fruit on top, flat sides down.

3   Beat together the remaining fat and sugar, add the eggs and beat again, then fold in the flour and spice. Spoon over the pears, peaches or pineapple and bake for 40–45 minutes.

4   Turn out onto a warmed serving plate and serve hot with custard (see page 92).

GOOSEBERRY FOOL

PREPARATION AND COOKING 1–1¼ HOURS
MAKES 5–6 HELPINGS

**2 lb/900 g gooseberries
½ pint/300 ml water
1 lb/450 g caster sugar
1 pint/600 ml double cream**

1   Place the gooseberries, water and half the sugar in a pan, and simmer very gently for 30–40 minutes until the fruit is tender. Push through a sieve and discard all the skin and pips. Add the remaining sugar to the purée and leave to cool.

2   Whip the cream – not too stiffly – and fold the purée gradually into it. Pour into a serving bowl.

POOR MAN'S

GOOSEBERRY FOOL

PREPARATION AND COOKING 1–1¼ HOURS
MAKES 5–6 HELPINGS

**2 lb/900 g gooseberries
½ pint/300 ml water
8 oz/225 g sugar
1 pint/600 ml custard (see page 92)**

1   Cook the gooseberries as for Gooseberry fool and sieve.

2   Make the custard, and while both gooseberry purée and custard are still warm, blend well together.

3   Pour into a serving dish and leave to cool.

Note: This recipe, and that for Gooseberry fool, can be made with other stewed fruits – rhubarb, apple, apricots etc.

SUMMER PUDDING

PREPARATION 30 MINUTES, PLUS OVERNIGHT SOAKING
MAKES 7–8 HELPINGS

1 lb/450 g redcurrants and blackcurrants
4 oz-100 g caster sugar
8 oz/250 g raspberries
8 slices white bread, crusts removed

1   Place the currants and sugar in a saucepan. Heat to a gentle simmer, and cook for 15–20 minutes, stirring occasionally until the fruits are tender. Add the raspberries and leave to cool. Strain off the juice and reserve.

2   Cut one piece of bread into two circles, one for the bottom of the basin and the other for the top (you may need two pieces if the basin is wide). Soak all the pieces of bread in the reserved fruit juice until they are evenly coloured.

3   Place the smaller bread circle in the bottom of the basin and line the sides with the other pieces, cutting them to fit where necessary. Pour in the fruit, then cover with the top circle.

4   Put a plate or saucer on top of the pudding with a heavy weight on top, about 1 lb/450 g (the plate must rest on the bread, not on the basin). Place in the refrigerator and leave overnight.

5   Turn out onto a serving dish and serve with whipped cream or warm custard (see page 92).

PLUM DUFF

PREPARATION 15 MINUTES, COOKING 2½–3 HOURS
MAKES 5–6 HELPINGS

**8 oz/225 g plain flour
1 teaspoon baking powder
Pinch of salt
3 oz/75 g shredded suet
1–1½ lb/450–675 g plums
2–3 oz/50–75 g granulated sugar**

1   Grease a 2-pint/1-litre pudding basin.

2   Sift the flour and baking powder together and add the suet and salt. Mix with enough cold water to make a soft but firm dough.

3   Roll out the dough to a thickness of about ½ in/1 cm and use to line the basin, leaving the spare dough hanging over the edge. Fill the basin with the fruit and sugar and a little water.

4   Bring the spare dough up over the top of the basin to enclose the fruit. Cut or pull off any spare dough. Dampen the edges and seal.

5   Place in a steamer over a pan of boiling water and cook for 2½–3 hours, topping up the boiling water when necessary. Turn carefully out onto a warmed serving dish and serve with custard (see page 92).

MOCK CHRISTMAS PUDDING

PREPARATION 30–40 MINUTES, COOKING 2 HOURS
MAKES 5–6 HELPINGS

**5 oz/125 g fresh brown or white breadcrumbs
¼ pint/150 ml milk and water, mixed
4 oz/100 g golden syrup
1½ oz/40 g butter or margarine
1 oz/25 g self-raising flour
2 teaspoons mixed spice
⅔ teaspoon bicarbonate of soda**

1   Grease a 2-pint/1-litre pudding basin.

2   Mix the breadcrumbs with the milk and water and leave to soak for 30 minutes. Beat with a fork.

3   Melt syrup and fat and stir into the breadcrumbs. Add flour, spice, bicarbonate of soda and fruit. If the mixture is too dry, add more milk.

4   Turn the mixture into the greased bowl, place in a steamer over a pan of boiling water, and steam for 2 hours, remembering to top up the pan of water from time to time.

PLUM PUDDING

(CHRISTMAS PUDDING)

PREPARATION 20–30 MINUTES COOKING 6–7 HOURS
MAKES 3 × 1 PINT/600 ML PUDDINGS

10 oz/275 g sultanas
10 oz/275 g currants
8 oz/225 g raisins
2 oz/50 g finely chopped almonds
1 teaspoon ground ginger
8 oz/225 g plain flour
Pinch of salt
1 lb/450 g soft brown sugar
8 oz/225 g finely chopped candied peel
1 teaspoon mixed spice
1 teaspoon grated nutmeg
8 oz/225 g breadcrumbs
10 oz/275 g shredded suet
6 eggs
4 tablespoons stout
Juice of 1 orange
1 wineglass brandy
About ½ pint/300 ml milk

1   Grease 3 × 1-pint/600-ml pudding basins.

2   Mix together the dry ingredients, fruit and spices. Beat the eggs well and mix with the stout, orange juice and brandy. Stir into the dry ingredients, adding enough milk to mix to a soft dropping consistency. Pour into the prepared basins.

3   Cover the basins with greaseproof paper and cloths and boil or steam for 6–7 hours. Remove the puddings from the boiling water or steamer and leave to cool. Cover each with a clean dry cloth and store in a cool dry place until required.

4   When required, boil or steam the pudding again for 1½–2 hours before serving. Serve with cream or brandy butter.

To make the brandy butter
3 oz/75 g butter, softened
oz/175 g icing sugar

Beat together the butter and sugar until light and fluffy. Work in the brandy and mix thoroughly. Store in the refrigerator until required.

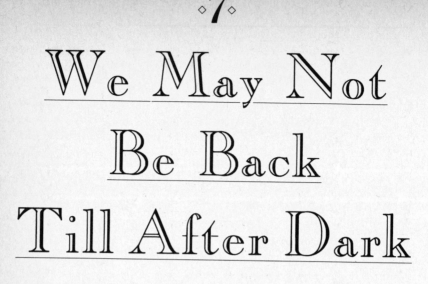

7

We May Not Be Back Till After Dark

THE chums set off with their rucksacks full of maps, compasses, water bottles, ropes, billycans, matches – and a more than adequate supply of food! As they marched along they reminisced about adventures and hikes they had enjoyed together and some of the scrapes they had got into.

'Do you recall that beastly day on the downs when we got ourselves so hopelessly lost?' asked Hardcastle. 'And those dratted cows that ran amok through our camp site in Cornwall!' laughed Caruthers. They chuckled too as they remembered the time they had rowed across to Squirrel Island for a spot of camping. They had had to mow down the nettles with their oars to get ashore; the paraffin from their lanterns had leaked all over the plum cake and sausages, and it rained so hard that they had spent the entire two-and-a-half days in rather damp clothing.

Nevertheless they had, on all occasions, had an absolutely ripping time, and they intended to enjoy today's expedition too. Certainly they would not go hungry: their provisions included a huge veal-and-ham pie, some Scotch eggs, a variety of sandwiches, flapjacks, a malt loaf, some toffee, packets of biscuits, oranges, apples, some bread pudding, and a few bottles of home-made ginger beer.

‘I hope we've brought enough food!’ said Morrell, ‘I'm feeling peckish already!’ ‘Oh dry up, Morrell,’ responded the others crossly, and Caruthers added, ‘No nosh yet; we've got a long day ahead, and we may not be back till after dark, so the supplies have got to last out.’

"I APPEAR TO HAVE LEFT YOUR SANDWICHES
BACK ON ALPHA IV, OLD MAN" HISSED BLAKE

COLD SAUSAGE
SANDWICHES

PREPARATION 5 MINUTES
MAKES 5 SANDWICHES

10 large sausages, cooked and cold
10 slices of buttered bread
Tomato relish

Spread half the slices of bread with tomato relish, then slice the sausages lengthwise and lay on top, using 2 for each round. Cover with the other slices of bread and press together firmly.

Alternatively, spread all the slices of bread with relish, place a whole sausage at one end of the slice and roll up inside the bread.

PEANUT BUTTER,
HONEY AND BANANA SANDWICHES

For each round, spread one slice of buttered granary bread with peanut butter, then carefully spread a layer of honey on top. Slice the banana and lay the slices on top of the honey.

Alternatively mash the banana and spread on top of the honey. Carefully cut in half or quarters.

SCOTCH EGGS

PREPARATION AND COOKING 25–30 MINUTES
MAKES 6

1 lb/450 g sausage meat
6 hard-boiled eggs, shelled
Freshly ground black pepper
Beaten egg
Golden breadcrumbs
Fat or oil for deep frying

1   Season the sausage meat with pepper and divide into 6 equal portions, then flatten each piece and use to wrap around each egg. Seal carefully so that the egg is completely enveloped, then coat with beaten egg and roll in the breadcrumbs.

2   Heat the oil or fat and fry the Scotch eggs until well browned. Remove from the pan and drain on kitchen towel. Leave to cool.

PORK PIE

PREPARATION 2¼–2½ HOURS, COOKING 2 HOURS
MAKES 6 HELPINGS

1 lb/450 g lean pork
1 teaspoon dried mixed herbs
Salt and freshly ground black pepper
1 small onion, finely chopped
4 tablespoons water or stock

For the pastry
8 oz/225 g plain flour, sifted
½ teaspoon salt
2½ oz/65 g lard
5–6 teaspoons water
Beaten egg to glaze

1   Cut the meat into small cubes and mix with the herbs, salt and pepper. Place the bones, onion and water or stock in a pan, season with salt and pepper, and simmer for 2 hours to make a good gravy that will form a jelly when cold.

2   Mix together the flour and salt. Place the lard and water in a pan and heat gently until the lard melts. Bring to the boil and pour into the flour. Mix thoroughly to make a soft paste. Turn onto a floured board.

3   Knead lightly for 2–3 minutes until smooth then, while it is still warm cut off one third and keep covered. Roll out the remaining pastry to a thickness of about ¼ in/6 mm and use to line a 6-in/15-cm pie dish or cake tin.

4   Heat the oven to Gas 7/220°C/425°F. Put the meat into the pie case and add a little stock. Roll out the remaining third of the pastry to form a lid. Dampen the edges and place over the pie, joining the edges carefully. Make a small hole in the centre and brush the top with beaten egg.

5   Bake for 15 minutes, then reduce the oven heat to Gas 4/180°C/ 350°F and bake for a further 1¼ hours. Remove from the oven, carefully lift out of dish or tin and brush the sides with beaten egg. Place on a baking tray and return to the oven for 30 minutes until the sides are golden. Remove from the oven and pour a little more warmed stock through the hole in the top. Leave to cool.

VEAL AND HAM PIE

PREPARATION AND COOKING 4 HOURS
MAKES 6–8 HELPINGS

12 oz/350 g stewing veal, trimmed of fat, and cut into small cubes
1 onion, finely chopped
Pinch of mace
Salt and freshly ground black pepper
Bouquet garni
1 lb/450 g ham, cut into small cubes
2 hard-boiled eggs, cut into thin slices

For the forcemeat balls
1 cup fresh white breadcrumbs
2 oz/50 g butter
1 egg
2 teaspoons mixed herbs (parsley, thyme, mint)

For the pastry
1 lb/450 g plain flour, sifted
1 teaspoon salt
5 oz/150 g lard, softened
6 fl oz/175 ml water
Beaten egg to glaze

For the aspic jelly
2 pints/1 litre veal stock, cooled, and all the fat removed
1 oz/25 g gelatine
Bouquet garni
2 sticks of celery, cut into large pieces
2 egg whites, lightly beaten
2 egg shells, washed and dried
1 glass sherry
8 tablespoons vinegar

1   Place the veal, onion, mace, bouquet garni, salt and pepper in a saucepan, cover with cold water and bring to the boil. Cook gently for about 2 hours until tender. Remove the bouquet garni and leave to cool.

2   Now make the aspic. Put into a pan all the ingredients except the sherry and vinegar, and whisk over the heat until nearly boiling. Add the sherry and vinegar and bring to the boil, whisking all the time. Reduce the heat and simmer for 10 minutes. Strain until clear.

3   Grease and line a 6-in/15-cm cake tin (with a loose bottom if possible.). Pre-heat the oven to Gas 7/220°C/425°F.

4   Mix together the flour and salt. Place the lard and water in a pan and heat gently until the lard melts. Bring to the boil and pour into the flour. Mix thoroughly to make a soft paste. Turn onto a floured board and knead lightly for 2–3 minutes until smooth.

5   While still warm, cut off one third of the pastry and keep covered. Roll out the remaining pastry to a thickness of ¼ in/6 mm and line the tin.

6   Now make the forcemeat balls. Rub the butter into the bread-crumbs. Add the herbs and egg, and mix thoroughly. Form into balls, roll in flour and drop into boiling stock for 5–10 minutes. Lift out carefully, drain and cool.

7   Cover the bottom of the pastry case with veal, then place a layer of ham on top. Add a few slices of egg. Sprinkle with a little lemon rind and lay a few forcemeat balls over.

8   Repeat the layers until the case is full. Roll out the remaining one-third of the pastry to form a lid. Dampen the edges with a little water and place the lid over the pie, pressing the edges firmly together. Make a hole in the middle and pour in some warm aspic. Brush the top with beaten egg.

9   Bake for 15 minutes, then reduce the oven to Gas 4/180°C/350°F and bake for a further 45–50 minutes until golden. Remove from the oven and carefully lift out of the cake tin. Place on a baking tray. Brush the sides with beaten egg and return to the oven for 20–30 minutes. Remove from the oven and pour a little more warm aspic through the hole in the top. Leave to cool.

Note: The aspic jelly can be made in advance and melted when needed.

SAUSAGE ROLLS

PREPARATION 15 MINUTES, COOKING 15 MINUTES
MAKES 8

**4 oz/100 g frozen puff pastry, thawed
8 oz/225 g sausage meat
Egg yolk to glaze**

1   Heat the oven to Gas 7/220°C/425°F and grease a baking tray.

2   Roll out the pastry on a floured board to a thickness of about ¼ in/6 mm and cut into 8 equal squares.

3   Divide the sausagemeat into 8 equal portions and form each one into a roll the same length as the pastry. Dampen the edges of the pastry with a little water and fold over the meat, leaving the ends open.

4   With a sharp knife, make 3 incisions on top, brush all over with beaten egg yolk and place on the baking tray. Bake for about 10 minutes until the pastry is golden and well risen. Reduce the oven heat to Gas 4/180°C/350°F and cook for a further 5 minutes.

SLICED MEAT LOAF

PREPARATION 10 MINUTES, COOKING 1½ HOURS
MAKES 6–8 HELPINGS

2 lb/900 g minced beef
2 small onions, chopped
2 teaspoons tomato purée
1 teaspoon creamed horseradish
6 oz/175 g fresh breadcrumbs, white or brown
Salt and freshly ground black pepper
¾ pint/425 ml stock

1   Pre-heat the oven to Gas 5/190°C/375°F and grease a 2-lb/900-g loaf tin.

2   Mix together all the ingredients, making sure that they are evenly distributed. Place in the prepared tin, smooth the top and bake for 1½ hours.

3   Remove from the oven, drain off excess juice and fat and leave the meat loaf to cool. Slice and wrap in foil or cling film. Serve between slices of crusty bread or in crusty rolls.

BOILED FRUIT LOAF

PREPARATION 25–30 MINUTES, COOKING 1¼–1½ HOURS

8 oz/225 g currants
8 oz/225 g sultanas
2 oz/50 g blanched almonds, chopped
2 oz/50 g glacé cherries, chopped
½ pint/300 ml water or cold tea
4 oz/100 g margarine
2 eggs
8 oz/225 g plain flour
1 teaspoon bicarbonate of soda
2 teaspoons mixed spice

1   Grease and line an 8-in/20-cm cake tin.

2   Place the fruit, nuts, water or cold tea and margarine in a pan, bring to the boil and boil for 1 minute. Remove from the heat and leave to cool.

3   Meanwhile heat the oven to gas 4/180°C/350°F. Beat the eggs into the fruit mixture. Mix together the flour, bicarbonate of soda and mixed spice and fold into the mixture.

4   Pour into the prepared tin and bake for 1¼–1½ hours until a skewer comes out clean. Remove from the oven, and turn out onto a wire rack. Leave to cool.

BREAD PUDDING

PREPARATION 1 HOUR (TO SOAK THE BREAD) PLUS 5 MINUTES, COOKING 1½–2 HOURS
MAKES ABOUT 8–9 SLABS

8 oz/225 g white or brown bread, crusts removed
3 oz/75 g soft brown sugar
3 oz/75 g currants
4 oz/100 g sultanas
4 oz/100 g raisins
2 eggs, beaten
8 tablespoons milk
1 teaspoon mixed spice or nutmeg
Grated rind of 1 lemon

1   Soak the bread in cold water for 1 hour then drain well.

2   Pre-heat the oven to Gas 4/180°C/350°F and grease a pie dish or a
6-in/13-cm square tin.

3   Mix the sugar, dried fruit, egg, milk, spice and lemon rind with
the bread. Turn into the prepared dish or tin and bake for 1½–2 hours.
Leave in the tin to become quite cold. Turn out and cut into slabs.

APPLE TURNOVERS

PREPARATION 10 MINUTES, COOKING 25–30 MINUTES
MAKES 8

12 oz/350 g plain flour, sifted
Pinch of salt
½ teaspoon baking powder
6 oz/175 g butter, softened
Cold water to mix
6 large apples, peeled, cored and thinly sliced
Ground cinnamon or cloves
2–3 tablespoons sugar
Beaten egg to glaze

1   Pre-heat the oven to Gas 5/190°C/375°F and grease a baking tray.

2   Mix together the flour, salt and baking powder, then rub in the
butter until the mixture resembles breadcrumbs. Add enough cold water
to mix to a soft but firm dough.

3   Roll out to a thickness of ¼ in/6 mm and cut into 8 circles. Divide
the apples between the pastry rounds, laying them on one half of the
dough. Sprinkle with a pinch of cinnamon or cloves and the sugar.

4   Wet the edges of the pastry with a little water, fold it over and pinch
the edges firmly together. Make a slit in the top of each. Brush all over
with beaten egg. Bake for 25–30 minutes until golden.

GINGER TORTE

PREPARATION 5 MINUTES (PLUS 5 MINUTES TO ICE) COOKING 20 MINUTES
MAKES 16 SQUARES

2 oz/50 g margarine or butter, softened
2 oz/50 g lard, softened
4 oz/100 g soft brown sugar
4 oz/100 g self-raising flour
1 teaspoon ground ginger
2 digestive biscuits, finely crumbled

For the icing
2 oz/50 g butter, softened
2 oz/50 g caster sugar
1 teaspoon ginger
2 teaspoons dried baby milk, such as Ostermilk

1   Pre-heat the oven to Gas 4/180°C/350°F and grease an 8-in/20-cm square cake tin.

2   Cream together the fat, lard and sugar, then work in the dry ingredients. Press into the prepared tin, smooth carefully, and bake for 20 minutes. Remove from the oven and leave in the tin to cool for 5 minutes, then cut into 16 squares.

3   For the icing, cream together the fat and sugar. Add the ginger and dried milk and mix well. Spread onto the top of each square and make a pattern with the prongs of a fork.

FLAPJACKS

PREPARATION 5 MINUTES, COOKING 25–30 MINUTES
MAKES 16 SQUARES

1 teaspoon demerara sugar
4 oz/100 g butter
4 oz/100 g golden syrup
6 oz/175 g rolled oats
A few drops of almond essence

1   Heat the oven to Gas 4/180°C/350°F and grease an 8-in/20-cm square cake tin.

2   Melt together the butter, sugar and syrup. Stir in the oats and almond essence. Press into the prepared tin and bake for 25–30 minutes until golden. Remove from the oven. Leave to cool for 4–5 minutes, then cut into 16 squares or fingers.

MALT LOAF

PREPARATION 20 MINUTES, COOKING 1½–1¾ HOURS

12 oz/350 g plain flour, sifted
Good pinch of salt
½ teaspoon bicarbonate of soda
1 teaspoon baking powder
1 teaspoon ground mixed spice
9 oz/250 g sultanas or raisins (or a mixture of both)
3 tablespoons demerara sugar
½ pint/300 ml malt extract
2 medium eggs, beaten
8 tablespoons milk

1   Pre-heat the oven to Gas 2/150°C/300°F and grease and line a 7-in/18-cm square cake tin. Grease the base of a baking tray large enough to cover the tin.

2   Mix together the flour, salt, soda, baking powder and spice in a bowl, then stir in the dried fruit.

3   In a pan, gently heat the sugar and malt extract, but do not boil. Pour the mixture into the dry ingredients and beat well.

4   Beat the eggs and gradually add with the milk, beating hard until the mixture is well blended. Pour into the prepared tin. Cover the tin with the baking tray, greased side down. Place an ovenproof weight on top and bake for 1½–¾ hours until a skewer comes out clean.

5   Remove from the oven and turn out onto a wire rack to cool. When cold, wrap in foil or clingfilm and store for 2–3 days before serving.

GINGER BEER

1 gallon/4.56 litres water
12 oz/350 g demerara sugar
1 oz/25 g bruised root ginger
2 oz/50 g cream of tartar
8 tablespoons fresh yeast

1   Bring the water to the boil, add the other ingredients and stir well together. Pour into an earthenware jug and cover with a cloth. Leave to cool. Add the yeast, stir well, cover and leave in a cool place overnight.

2   Carefully remove all the scum which has risen to the top, then pour into clean bottles. The bottles must be tightly corked or stoppered – then left for 3–4 days. The ginger beer will then be ready.

Midnight
Feasts

IT WAS A DEVICE FOR TURNING SCHOOL MEALS
BACK INTO FOOD

ONE morning, three weeks after the chums had returned to Mannington, the school carrier brought Patterson a large hamper from home. Being the sort of chap who always liked to do the right thing, he invited his four best and most intimate friends to a supper party in the pavilion at the far end of the playing field.

'It's a bit risky, isn't it?' asked Morrell. 'No fear', replied Patterson confidently. 'We can't possibly be heard from the school, as it's too far away and we shan't need the lights on as there's a full moon tonight! If we stay low in the locker room no one will see us.' 'It'll be safe enough,' agreed Bennett, knowing that once they were on the other side of the drive all would be well.

Late that night, the five adventurers carefully lowered the hamper to the ground from the window of the dorm and then descended by means of a rope. Silently they moved towards the playing field, keeping carefully to the shadows cast by the tall trees.

Once safely inside the pavilion, they opened the hamper to survey the mouth-watering contents. There was a huge plum cake, a packet of home-made fudge, a pork pie, jars of chutney and preserved ginger, corned beef, sardines, half a dozen mince pies, a chicken and huge treacle tart.

Caruthers produced some chocolate and a jar of Marmite; Bennett emptied butterscotch and slices of bread from his pockets; Morrell had concealed cooked sausages and a jar of jam under his coat and Hardcastle's contribution to the spread was a bag full of rum truffles and a flask of steaming hot cocoa.

'What a jape!' said Hardcastle, 'good old Mater. She always packs first-rate nosh. Let's tuck into the chicken first! Here, Caruthers, how about knocking up some Marmite sandwiches as well. This is gong to be a real feast!'

CHEESE DREAMS

PREPARATION AND COOKING 10–15 MINUTES
MAKES 6 SANDWICHES

12 slices of buttered bread
10 oz/375 g mature Cheddar, sliced or grated
Fat or oil for frying

1   Lay the cheese on half of the slices of bread and press the others down on top to make 6 firm sandwiches.

2   Heat the fat or oil in a frying pan and fry the sandwiches, turning carefully, until golden brown on both sides.

MARMITE SANDWICHES

Spread Marmite quite thinly on buttered bread and sandwich together with more buttered bread.

Also delicious are cheese and Marmite, peanut butter and Marmite, cucumber and Marmite!

SAUSAGES AND BACON

ON STICKS

PREPARATION AND COOKING 20–25 MINUTES
MAKES 16

8 thin sausages
16 rashers of bacon
16 cocktail sticks

1   Cut each sausage in half and grill under a slow heat until just beginning to brown.

2   Remove from the heat and wrap a rasher of bacon around each sausage. Place back under the grill and cook until the bacon is well crisped. Turn the rolls frequently to ensure they cook through.

3   Remove from the heat and leave to cool. Stick a cocktail stick in each.

BROKEN BISCUIT CAKE

PREPARATION 10 MINUTES

4 oz/50 g margarine or butter
1 heaped tablespoon golden syrup
2–3 oz/50–75 g sultanas or raisins
4 tablespoons drinking chocolate powder
8 oz/225 g digestive biscuits, crumbed

1   Grease a 7-in/18-cm round sandwich tin.

2   Heat together the fat, syrup and dried fruit until the fat has melted. Add the chocolate powder and stir well.

3   Stir in the crumbed biscuits, mix well and turn into the prepared tin. Smooth the top and leave to set in the refrigerator.

BUTTERSCOTCH

Bennett has a veritable weakness for butterscotch, and as a small child had constantly sticky trouser-pockets as a result of his insistence on always having a supply handy. As he has grown older he has become a touch more careful, and always makes quite sure that his portable supply is well wrapped!

•

PREPARATION AND COOKING 30–40 MINUTES
MAKES 36 PIECES

1 lb/450 g demerara sugar
8 tablespoons water
2 teaspoons lemon juice
2 oz/50 g butter

1   Oil a 7-in/18-cm square cake tin.

2   Place the sugar, water and lemon juice in a strong saucepan and heat slowly, stirring all the time, until the sugar has dissolved.

3   Add the butter and bring the mixture to the boil. Brush down the sides of the saucepan with a brush dipped in water to dissolve any sugar left on the sides of the pan.

4   Boil the mixture to 138°C/280°F. Keep checking for 'set' by dropping a little of the mixture into cold water. If ready, the mixture will set and become brittle.

5   When setting point is reached pour immediately into the prepared tin, and, as it begins to set, mark into squares with a blunt knife. Leave to cool and harden.

6   Remove from the tin, break into pieces and wrap in greaseproof paper.

Hard Toffee

PREPARATION AND COOKING 20–30 MINUTES
MAKES 36 PIECES

8 tablespoons water
1 lb/450 g granulated sugar
1 tablespoon golden syrup
2 teaspoons lemon juice or vinegar
2 oz/50 g butter

1   Grease a 7-in/18-cm square cake tin.

2   Heat the water and sugar gently together, stirring all the time, until the sugar has dissolved.

3   Add the syrup, lemon juice or vinegar, and butter. Bring to the boil and boil to 155.5°C/312°F. Test for 'set' by removing the pan from the heat and placing a little of the mixture in a saucer of cold water. If ready, it will set hard and brittle. Quickly pour into the prepared tin and mark into squares when it begins to harden.

4   When cold, break into pieces and wrap in greaseproof paper.

Fudge

PREPARATION 10–15 MINUTES
MAKES ABOUT 36 PIECES

8 tablespoons milk
1 small can condensed milk
4 oz/100 g butter
1 rounded tablespoon golden syrup
1 lb/400 g granulated sugar
Pinch of cream of tartar
½ teaspoon vanilla essence

1   Grease a shallow 7-in/18-cm square cake tin.

2   Place all the ingredients in a heavy pan and slowly bring to the boil, stirring continuously until dissolved.

3   Boil quickly, stirring occasionally, to 115.5°C/240°F, and test for 'set' by dropping a little of the mixture into cold water. If ready it will form a soft ball.

4   Remove from the heat and beat until thick. Pour quickly into the tin. Leave until almost set, then cut into squares. When cool, remove from the tin and leave on a rack to harden.

CHOCOLATE ORANGE FUDGE

PREPARATION AND COOKING 10 MINUTES
MAKES ABOUT 48 PIECES

**4 oz/100 g plain chocolate
2 oz/50 g butter
Grated rind of 1 orange
4 tablespoons evaporated milk
12 oz/325 g icing sugar**

1   Grease a 7-in/18-cm square cake tin. Melt the chocolate and butter together in a bowl over hot water. Add the orange rind and evaporated milk and mix well.

2   Work in the sugar and stir until stiff. Put into the prepared tin and leave to set. Cut into squares.

COCONUT PYRAMIDS

PREPARATION 10 MINUTES, COOKING 1 HOUR
MAKES 18

**Rice paper
3 egg whites
1½ oz/40 g rice flour
4–5 oz/100–125 g caster sugar
8 oz/225 g desiccated coconut
½ teaspoon vanilla essence**

1   Pre-heat the oven to Gas 2/100°C/310°F and place sheets of rice paper ready on baking trays.

2   Whisk the egg whites very stiffly. Lightly stir in the rice flour, sugar, coconut and vanilla. Place in small close heaps on the rice paper.

3   Bake for 1 hour until light brown. Remove from the oven and leave to cool.

RUM TRUFFLES

PREPARATION AND COOKING 40–45 MINUTES
MAKES 10–12

6 oz/175 g plain chocolate
2 teaspoons rum
1 egg yolk
1 oz/25 g butter, softened
1 teaspoon single cream
Chocolate vermicelli for coating

1 Melt the chocolate in a bowl over hot water. Beat in the rum, egg yolk, butter and cream, and leave to cool for about 30 minutes.

2 When cool, roll into balls and coat in vermicelli.

PLUM CAKE

PREPARATION 15–20 MINUTES, COOKING 2¼–2½ HOURS

10 oz/275 g caster sugar
4 oz/100 g butter, softened
4 eggs, beaten
12 oz/350 g plain flour
¾ teaspoon baking powder
4 oz/100 g sultanas
8 oz/250 g currants
3 oz/75 g candied peel
3 oz/75 g ground almonds
7½ fl oz/200 ml milk

1 Pre-heat the oven to Gas 3/170°C/325°F and grease and line an 8-in/20-cm round cake tin.

2 Cream together the sugar and butter until light and fluffy. Add the eggs, a little at a time, beating well after each addition.

3 Mix together the flour and baking powder. Add to the mixture and stir thoroughly. Add the dried fruit, ground almonds and milk and mix well together.

4 Turn into the prepared tin and bake for 2¼–2½ hours. Remove from the oven and leave to cool in the tin for 15 minutes, then turn out onto a wire rack and leave to cool completely.

TREACLE TART

PREPARATION 30–40 MINUTES INCLUDING 15 MINUTES FOR CHILLING THE PASTRY,
COOKING 30–40 MINUTES
MAKES 5–6 HELPINGS

For the rough puff pastry
6 oz/125 g plain flour
4½ oz/115 g butter, softened
½ teaspoon lemon juice
Cold water to mix

For the filling
3–4 tablespoons golden syrup
1 teaspoon lemon juice or ½ teaspoon ground ginger
3 oz/75 g fresh breadcrumbs

1   Grease an 8-in/20-cm ovenproof plate.

2   Mix together the flour and salt. Cut the butter into small pieces the size of a walnut, and mix lightly into the flour. Add the lemon juice and just enough water to mix to an elastic dough.

3   On a floured surface, roll out the pastry into a long strip, keeping the corners square, and fold into three. Seal the edges with the rolling pin and give the pastry a half-turn so that the folded edges are on your right and left. Repeat until the pastry has been rolled and folded four times – if possible leaving for 15 minutes in the refrigerator between the second and third rollings.

4   Meanwhile heat the oven to Gas 5/190°C/375°F. Roll out the pastry again to a thickness of about ¼ in/6 mm and use to line the prepared plate. Trim the edge. Cut strips from the spare pastry, dampen the edges and lay on top of the rim to give a double layer. Decorate by pressing a knife blade all around.

5   Warm the syrup, flavour with the lemon juice or ginger and stir in the breadcrumbs. Spoon into the pastry case, decorate with criss-cross strips of pastry and bake for 30–40 minutes. Serve hot or cold with custard or cream.

COCOA

THE FOLLOWING QUANTITIES ARE FOR EACH MUG OF COCOA

½ pint/300 ml milk
1½ teaspoon cocoa powder
1 teaspoon sugar (or to taste)

1   Mix the cocoa powder and sugar with a little of the milk to a smooth paste. Bring the rest of the milk to the boil.

2   Pour the boiling milk onto the paste, stirring all the time. Mix well.

Index